DODGERS
ESSENTIAL

DODGERS ESSENTIAL

Everything You Need to Know to Be a Real Fan!

Steven Travers

TRIUMPH
BOOKS

Library of Congress Cataloging-in-Publication Data

Travers, Steven.
    Dodgers essential : everything you need to know to be a real fan! / Steven Travers.
        p. cm.
    Includes bibliographical references.
    ISBN-13: 978-1-57243-942-9 (hard cover)
    ISBN-10: 1-57243-942-4 (hard cover)
    1. Brooklyn Dodgers (Baseball team)—History. 2. Los Angeles Dodgers (Baseball team)—History. I. Title.

GV875.B7T72 2007
796.357'640979494—dc22
[B]

                                                                2006031767

This book is available in quantity at special discounts for your group or organization. For further information, contact:

Triumph Books
542 South Dearborn Street
Suite 750
Chicago, Illinois 60605
(312) 939-3330
Fax (312) 663-3557

Printed in U.S.A.
ISBN: 978-1-57243-942-9
Design by Patricia Frey
All photos courtesy of AP/Wide World Photos except where otherwise indicated

To my daughter, Elizabeth Travers.
I'll always remember the look on
your face at Dodger Stadium when
I caught Eddie Murray's home run
and gave the ball to you.

Contents

Foreword

Walter Francis O'Malley appeared before the Los Angeles City Council in 1957 seeking permission to play four seasons at the Los Angeles Memorial Coliseum while Dodger Stadium was being built.

There was one dissenter.

Councilman John Holland was opposed to the idea. It turned out that Holland was in league with C. Arnholt Smith of San Diego. Smith wanted the franchise for himself and later went to prison for fraud.

Then there were "the Squatters," as O'Malley called them. The Arechiga family lived in Chavez Ravine rent- and tax-free. They were displaced, and to this day there are those who feel they were dealt with unfairly, especially the Arechigas.

The Ravine, located in Sulpher Canyon, was a desolate place, with garbage strewn everywhere, empty beer cans aplenty. Some used it as a "lovers' lane."

One of the great aerial views in sports today is Dodger Stadium. O'Malley ordered the planting of trees and flowers.

The Los Angeles Angels played there four seasons, 1962 through 1965, while Anaheim Stadium was being built. The Angels insisted that all datelines out of Dodger Stadium be listed as "Chavez Ravine."

This had to be confusing to readers and television viewers because Chavez Ravine seemed to be a carbon copy of Dodger Stadium. Two clubs using the same venue has never worked. Angels owner Gene Autry knew he had to move. Team president Bob Reynolds negotiated a lease with Anaheim, and the Angels moved in 1966.

Dodger Stadium underwent a facelift in 2006. Current owner Frank McCourt replaced every seat and every seat foundation. The original color scheme was restored. It's back to yellow field boxes, orange loge level, green reserved seats, and red for the general admission section at the top.

I find it as attractive as the day it opened.

I sat in Peter O'Malley's office in 1996 when the family sold the team to Fox Corporation.

And I swore I would never go back.

But I did early in the '06 season and will return for more games.

In fact, Peter says, "Let me know the next time you attend a game and I'll go with you."

Other stadiums rely on gimmicks to pry even more money from the customers with video games, etc. All they sell at Dodger Stadium is baseball, souvenirs, and good food. Of course, the cost of beer is outrageous at $8.50 a cup. Sales are cut off after the seventh inning for obvious reasons.

So some things change and other things stay the same. One thing that has stayed the same is the talent and loyalty of my friend Steve Travers. I first met Steve in the 1990s, when he had written a screenplay based on the life of my old Angel pal Bo Belinsky. Steve wanted my help for research and also to promote the project, which I was happy to do.

Since then Steve has become a prolific writer, one of the best in the business. His latest book, *Dodgers Essential: Everything You Need to Know to Be a Real Fan!* is a great look back at Dodger history. He gives it to you straight, filled with homage to all the things that make Dodger baseball great: Jackie Robinson, Branch Rickey, Sandy Koufax, Steve Garvey, and, of course, Vin Scully, just to name a few.

I'm glad Steve asked me to write this foreword, because I hope I was able to pass my love of baseball and the Dodgers to younger writers like him, who are now carrying the torch.

—Bud "the Steamer" Furillo

Bud Furillo migrated to Los Angeles while still a high school student, ascending to a place among the all-time greatest sports personalities in Southland history.

As sports editor of the L.A. Herald-Examiner, *"the Steamer"—so named because his columns were called "In the Steam Room"—not only covered every great team and player in Los Angeles, but he befriended them in ways that nobody does anymore. In the 1980s he hosted* Dodgertalk *on KABC.*

There is no greater authority on Dodgers baseball. Bud passed away in July 2006. This foreword is his last published work.

Acknowledgments

Thanks to Tom Bast, Jess Paumier, Amy Reagan, Kelley White, Linc Wonham, and all the great folks at Triumph Books and Random House Publishing for having faith in me. Thanks also to my agent, Craig Wiley. I want to thank the Dodgers, a class organization all the way. Thanks also to Pat Kelly and John Horne of the Baseball Hall of Fame. Thanks to Peter Miller and the late, great Bud Furillo. Thank you to Karen Peterson for web assistance. To Donna Carter, Tommy Lasorda, Rick Monday, Vin Scully, Chad Kreuter, and Ross Porter: thanks.

Hey, thanks to Jake Downey and Mike McDowd, great Dodger fans. Mike, you do a fine "Vin Scully." Of course, my thanks as always go out to my daughter, Elizabeth Travers; my parents, Don and Inge Travers; and to my Lord and savior, Jesus Christ, who has shed his grace on thee, and to whom all glory is due!

Introduction

Radio 640 KFI out of Los Angeles carried Dodger baseball until 1973, which meant the voice of Vin Scully. Memories: vacation trips to the mountains, huddled close to a crackling radio with my dad. The dulcet Irish tones of the great Scully against the backdrop of a black-forest night...

"And that brings up Ted Sizemore..."

Beyond our little place, the hoots of mountain creatures mixed with Scully.

"Walter Alston's gonna go out and have a chat with Sutton..."

Up in the sky, away from the L.A. smog, a billion stars illuminated the August night.

"And that's why Willie Davis won the Gold Glove award..."

Oh, Vin Scully. A poet. A baseball Shakespeare. Without peer, the *greatest sports announcer who ever lived,* so help me God.

If you want to know what makes America great, well, there are a lot of reasons. I give all due credit to God, the constitution, our military, the capitalist system, the three-branch system of government, the Puritan work ethic...but brother, I'm tellin' ya, the emotional attachment of father and son to the game of baseball is as uniquely American as any of those other concepts. I know they have soccer in Germany, ice hockey in Canada, and fathers watch with sons. And I love my Southern Cal Trojans in college football, and before I went to USC, I dug John Wooden's Bruins. But *nothing* compares to baseball.

There's a poster that hangs in my favorite sports bar that reads, "The effect of bat on ball, that's physics. The effect of baseball on America...that's *chemistry,* my friend." The effect of Scully and the

Dodgers on the city of Los Angeles? That's a marriage made in heaven. Scully is the most valuable Dodger of all time, which is saying something.

When I was attending the University of Southern California, my baseball pals and I were constantly making the short drive to Dodger Stadium. USC is close enough that you do not have to take a freeway to get there. One time my buddies Chris Wildermuth and Terry Marks were driving there, taking the Sunset Boulevard route. Pregame traffic was heavy. Chris saw an opening and spurted forward ahead of a Cadillac. Then he looked in the mirror.

"Oh my God," he exclaimed, "I just cut off Vin Scully."

Terry and I turned and waved profusely at Vin, asking that he forgive us our sins, and with the benevolent wave of his hand, like a friendly Irish Catholic priest, he did so, accompanied by a pleasant smile.

I pitched in the best high school baseball program in California. In fact, we were the best in the entire *country,* actually being named the prep national champions my senior year. We did get tripped up one time, though. We took an undefeated record down to San Diego to play Point Loma, Hoover, and Lincoln. The day after we dispatched Point Loma, we arrived at Ted Williams Field, Hoover High's facility, which was named after their great alum. We led Hoover 5–3 in the bottom of the last inning. Then they pushed a run across, had two men on, and their best hitter at the plate.

That hitter? Mike Davis, the man Dennis Eckersley walked *to get to* Kirk Gibson in Game 1 of the 1988 World Series. On this spring day Davis was the hero, blasting a double off the giant image of a St. Louis–style "Cardinal" on the right-center-field scoreboard to win it, 6–5. In the second game we defeated Lincoln handily, but their third baseman impressed us with his athleticism. That was Marcus Allen.

Mike Davis was not the only future Dodger we faced. In the California State Joe DiMaggio League Tournament, we played against the Long Beach Jets, composed of guys mainly from Poly High. Both Gwynns, Tony and Chris (Dodgers: 1987–91, 1994–95), played for the

Jets. In college I remember a fall ballgame against a hard-throwing lefty from Santa Barbara City College named Bob Ojeda.

I signed with the St. Louis Cardinals and pitched in their organization for a year, but there were no Dodger farm clubs in the league I played in. The next season I was with the Oakland Athletics. We trained in Arizona and never saw the Dodgers, who were in Florida. But I was sent to Modesto of the Class A California League. I was throwing batting practice on a hot afternoon when the Lodi Dodgers traipsed into our ballpark for the first of a three-game series. I cannot even recall any big names, but I sure remember that Dodger blue. Don't ask me why, but it looked different from Giant orange, Twin purple, and Padre brown. Only Yankee pinstripes and Cardinal red has the same effect, in my opinion.

I lasted about a week in Modesto, but I saw the Dodgers again, this time as a member of the Idaho Falls A's when we traveled to Lethbridge, Alberta, Canada, of the Pioneer League. It's about as far from Dodger Stadium, physically and mentally, as it gets, but *still,* the Dodger series had the effect of being more intense than all others. I managed to get into a beanball war with those guys. One of the Dodgers was a young shortstop from the Dominican Republic named Mariano Duncan. A couple of our players got hit, I had to go after somebody, then *boom!* An on-field brawl. I just remember seeing a bunch of those blue-and-white uniforms heading out of their dugout toward me and thinking to myself, *Hey guys, I'm a Dodger fan!*

Being on the team facing the Dodgers, I saw just how much their opponents wanted to beat them. It's a special feeling, more competitive than most of the teams we faced.

Baseball is like that sometimes. I feel badly for folks who have never really experienced the camaraderie, the intensity and passion of the game, the rivalry, the competition.

Trolley Dodgers

In the Big Inning, there was baseball, and it was good! A history of the Dodgers is a history of baseball, going back to its roots. Its roots are in New York. We all know the story. An Army officer, Abner Doubleday, "invents" baseball in upstate New York. Semi-uniformed privates, sergeants, and captains make up the first teams. Maybe they did play some ball at Cooperstown in 1839, but we now know the story is at least as mythological as factual.

But Doubleday became a general and a Civil War hero. His legacy had legs, and so he got the credit for a game that really started with cricket and rounders, came here from England, and developed from there.

The first professional team was in Cincinnati, but the game was popularized in New York City, where teams would gather to play on the aptly named Elysian Fields. The National League started in 1876. New York City was a charter member. In 1882 the American Association was formed.

Brooklyn entered the American Association in 1884, but early origins of what exactly constituted the Dodger franchise are some-what sketchy. The first Brooklyn club, the Atlantics, was "national champion" in the 1860s. A later Brooklyn club comprised of dock-workers and day laborers also existed. Then the Atlantics emerged as a franchise in the American Association. The leagues were at war with each other. Franchises came and went, switched cities and names. Allegiances were ephemeral. The Dodger media guide lists the first team as 1890, but Brooklyn fielded teams in both the National League and American Association before that.

1

DID YOU KNOW ... That Dodger manager Ned Hanlon, considered the master of the "little game," produced such successful future managers as John McGraw, Hughie Jennings, and Wilbert Robinson?

Right from the beginning, Brooklyn and its baseball team suffered from an inferiority complex. The New York franchise had panache. Owner Jim Mutrie dubbed them with their lasting nickname when he observed them and noted wistfully, "My Giants." Since New York City was already a giant city, the new kingpin of world commerce in the late 19th century, the nickname was apropos.

But, the Giants did not actually play in Manhattan. Over the years, the Giants, Yankees, and football Giants were called "Manhattan's team," as opposed to teams toiling away in Brooklyn, Long Island, Flushing Meadows, and New Jersey.

But Brooklyn *never* had grandeur or glamour attached to it. At first it was a separate unincorporated borough from New York, located across the river. A suburb. New York decided to incorporate all its boroughs into a single, huge city. Against much political opposition, Brooklyn was made a part of New York, the same way the San Fernando Valley would later be swallowed up by Los Angeles.

In 1883 the Brooklyn Bridge was completed, inexorably tying Brooklyn to New York City. Whether by car, subway, or on foot, the distance between lower Manhattan and Brooklyn became small in distance, but remained large in public perception. Brooklynites never lost the sense that they were looked down upon. This would fuel rivalries with the Giants and, eventually, the Yankees.

The name "Dodgers" came about via an evolutionary process. The Brooklyn franchises went at various times by names the Atlantics, Robins, and Superbas. Their fans would take the subway train to the park and cross the street. Trolley cars traversed the area, so the fans had to have their wits about them in order to avoid injury. It was a "hustle and bustle" scene of trolleys, horses, buggies, people, bicycles, and eventually cars. This environment resulted in pundits referring to their fans as "Trolley Dodgers." This eventually became "Dodgers." Over time many have attributed other reasons to the name. The "Artful Dodger" of *Oliver Twist* fame, for instance, led some to believe the team was named after a street hustler, a pseudo thief, but the trolley story is the legitimate origin of the now world-famous moniker.

Brooklyn was a junior partner in baseball's New York firm, a well-placed second to the mighty Giants. But it is worth noting that they were, if not a thriving organization, and maybe not even a well-established one, nevertheless a major league baseball team in good standing long before the New York Yankees were a glint in anybody's eye. The Yankees were not even the Yankees for the first decade or so of their existence.

They were the Highlanders. They played in a chintzy little ball-park, swallowing their pride and renting out the Polo Grounds from the Giants until Yankee Stadium was built in 1923. In Brooklyn a "major league" baseball team was plying its trade in one way or another for 11 years before Babe Ruth was even born.

The Brooklyn Bridge, built in 1883, was the first step toward incorporating Brooklyn into New York City, but the borough always remained an "outsider," as did its baseball team.

3

The American League came about in 1901. By the early 20th century, the two leagues were established, their disputes more or less settled. Eight-team leagues were formed. Those franchises existed in stability through years of a brief, threatening third league (the Federal League) and two world wars, until the 1950s franchise shifts of Boston to Milwaukee, Philadelphia to Kansas City, New York to San Francisco, and Brooklyn to Los Angeles.

Brooklyn set no houses afire, although they were not as bad as popular history paints them. The so-called "first" Brooklyn franchise, the one with direct National League lineage to the royal family of Walter O'Malley, Sandy Koufax, and Tommy Lasorda, actually won the 1890 pennant under manager William McGunnigle. But under future Hall of Famer John Montgomery Ward, the Brooklyns of 1891 slumped to 61–76. The schizophrenia continued in 1892 when Ward turned the team around with a 95–59 mark. C.H. Ebbets was the team's third manager, of the disappointing 1898 team that finished 54–91. He had the good sense to give up his brief career as field skipper to Ned Hanlon, who won the 1899 and 1900 pennants, sticking around through the 1905 campaign.

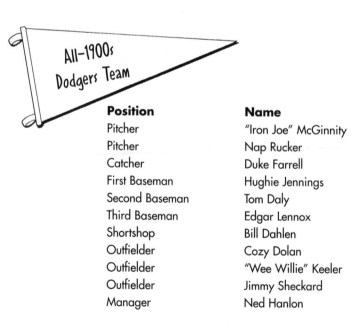

All-1900s Dodgers Team

Position	Name
Pitcher	"Iron Joe" McGinnity
Pitcher	Nap Rucker
Catcher	Duke Farrell
First Baseman	Hughie Jennings
Second Baseman	Tom Daly
Third Baseman	Edgar Lennox
Shortshop	Bill Dahlen
Outfielder	Cozy Dolan
Outfielder	"Wee Willie" Keeler
Outfielder	Jimmy Sheckard
Manager	Ned Hanlon

Unfortunately, pennants won before 1903 have virtually no imprimatur in the hierarchy of baseball respect. They are viewed as ancient history, like the multiple "national championships" won by Harvard and Yale before World War I. The American and National Leagues began playing each other in the World Series in 1903, an experiment that has worked out pretty well (with the exception of 1904, when the Giants refused to play the "busher" Boston Pilgrims, *née* Red Sox).

TRIVIA

How many Brooklyn Dodgers of the decade 1900–09 were elected to the Baseball Hall of Fame?

Answers to the trivia questions are on pages 178–179

Baseball was a thriving professional sport for 34 years before 1903. The National League had been a success since 1876. The American Association is regarded by history as a "major" league, but it was not given true status. Its successor, the American League, was not respected at first. Then the first World Series was played and won by its champions, Boston (with a pretty fair pitcher named Cy Young). The team that New York Giants manager John McGraw called "bushers" had beaten the Pittsburgh Pirates of Honus Wagner.

So Brooklyn's championships prior to the World Series era are therefore relegated to the hieroglyphics of the so-called "pre-modern era." In the new age they suffered badly at the hands of McGraw's Giants, Wagner's Pirates, and the fabulous Chicago Cubs of Tinker-to-Evers-to-Chance double-play fame.

Wilbert Robinson Plants the Seed of a Baseball Tree That Grew in Brooklyn

Year after year, Brooklyn existed as little more than cannon fodder for the Giants, Pirates, and Cubs. Some of baseball's immortal names graced the diamonds of pre–World War I America: Christy Mathewson of the Giants, Honus Wagner of the Pirates, and Grover Cleveland Alexander of the Phillies. In the American League, there were the likes of Ty Cobb in Detroit, the infamous "Shoeless Joe" Jackson in Chicago, and Walter Johnson in Washington.

Brooklyn? They had "Wee Willie" Keeler, a Hall of Fame singles hitter who "hit 'em where they ain't;" there was Nap Rucker, a pretty fair "country pitcher," as they said, who sported a 22–18 record in 1911; and infielder Jake Daubert, an excellent ball player. But the seeds of baseball greatness began to take root in Brooklyn in 1911 (when young Zack Wheat broke into the starting line-up), in 1913 (when the ridiculous Superbas nickname was gratefully lost to history, although "Dodgers" did not officially stick), and in 1914, when "Uncle Wilbert" Robinson took the reigns as manager of the so-called "Robins."

Robinson brought respectability to Brooklyn. Over the next two years, baseball went through more growing pains. War raged in Europe, but President Woodrow Wilson promised to keep America out of the conflict. The Federal League opened up for business, stealing big-name players such as Philadelphia A's pitching ace Chief Bender. By 1916, however, the Federal League had folded.

The long-suffering Brooklyn Atlantics-Robins-Superbas-Trolley Dodgers-Dodgers finally won the National League pennant in 1916. It was the result of many years of painstaking hard work on the part of their owner, one Charles Hercules Ebbets. He rose by the sweat of his brow—in the greatest of American traditions—from ticket-taker to baseball magnate. He was rewarded with shares of team stock for his work as club secretary, was elected team president in 1898, and moved the franchise to south Brooklyn, where he built a new version of the old Washington Park.

Ebbets borrowed heavily from Wall Street to keep up with the thriving Giants and American League Highlanders (later Yankees). But in 1913, he solidified his hold on the franchise, his name in history, and the club's place in the hearts of Brooklynites when his Ebbets Field was completed.

It was, by the standards of the day, a baseball palace, built on a vacant lot in the Bedford-Stuyvesant (known as Bed-Stuy) section of Flatbush. Ebbets Field was a bandbox by later standards, unable to contain the offensive exploits of Roy Campanella and Duke Snider, but in the "dead-ball era" of 1913 it was just right.

In 1912 outfielder Casey Stengel broke in with Brooklyn. In 1916 Stengel hit .364, but apparently lacked confidence in the team's ability to defeat Babe Ruth and the mighty Boston Red Sox in the World Series. He casually inquired of his teammates what they planned to do with their *loser's* share of the fall classic's gate receipts.

Wilbert Robinson was the face of Brooklyn baseball before, during, and after World War I.

7

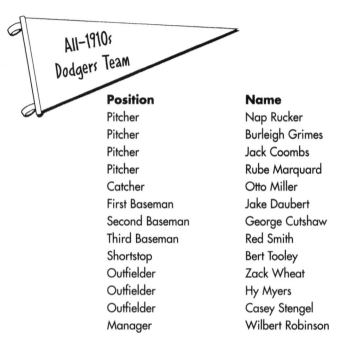

All-1910s Dodgers Team

Position	Name
Pitcher	Nap Rucker
Pitcher	Burleigh Grimes
Pitcher	Jack Coombs
Pitcher	Rube Marquard
Catcher	Otto Miller
First Baseman	Jake Daubert
Second Baseman	George Cutshaw
Third Baseman	Red Smith
Shortstop	Bert Tooley
Outfielder	Zack Wheat
Outfielder	Hy Myers
Outfielder	Casey Stengel
Manager	Wilbert Robinson

But it was Wilbert Robinson who turned Ebbets's team into winners—not a dynasty but a competitive ball club. Robinson's baseball reputation is one of a cross between a clown (not unlike Stengel's) and a kindly uncle. He was dubbed "Uncle Wilbert" and then "Uncle Robbie" by writer Damon Runyon, who knew characters when he saw them.

But Robinson was a first-class baseball man, a former Brooklyn catcher who cut his teeth as John McGraw's third-base coach and "pitching coach" (a loose affiliation before such coaches really existed) with New York. But during a drunken bash following the disappointing 1913 loss to Philadelphia in the World Series, McGraw and Robinson had an argument. Robinson was fired, and Ebbets hired him.

The Robinson image would propel the Dodgers' reputation into that of a laughingstock—Robins, Bums, "Daffiness Boys." There were reasons for this. For one, the Dodger uniforms were less than regal; a kind of checkerboard look with a "B" on the chest that did not match up to Yankee pinstripes and the well-known "NY" insignia of the Giants' and Yanks' caps.

Robinson, like Stengel, was something of a John Candy character. There was a comic quality to his appearance, to his roly-poly body, his rubbery face. He need not say anything. He just *looked* funny.

Part of Robinson's "clown act" reputation resulted from a spring-training incident in 1916. The airplane was a new innovation. The record for a dropped baseball was 504 feet, from the top of the Washington Monument. Ebbets decided to break that record by dropping a ball from a plane. Robinson was advised not to fly due to ill health, which does not explain the folly of his decision to *catch* the hurtling sphere, which, dropped from over 500 feet out of a plane traveling 45 mph, could kill him if he missed it!

Aviatrix Ruth Law flew over the park, but she had forgotten the baseball in her hotel room. She brought a grapefruit instead, unbeknownst to Uncle Robbie, waiting in full catcher's gear while his team gave him a wide berth. The grapefruit splattered into his glove, covering his chest protector with juice and pulp. Robinson was knocked flat, and quickly felt the warm liquid.

"Jesus, I'm hit!" announced Robinson as if he had taken German machine-gun fire at the Somme. He said, "Help me, lads, I'm covered with my own blood." Then Robinson opened his eyes, noticed it was grapefruit juice, not blood, and his players bowled over in laughter. Casey Stengel took "credit" for the grapefruit, claiming to have replaced the ball with it.

Robinson managed to profit from other team's losses from Federal League "raids," picking up star players in the twilight of their careers. Rube Marquard, a Hall of Fame lefty for McGraw's Giants, came over and won 13 games. Another ex-Giant star, catcher Chief Meyers, made the move to Brooklyn.

Stengel, a true character, had a dismal 1915 season. According to rumor, he was recovering from venereal disease. Back up to speed in 1916, he was a key player. First baseman Jake Daubert, one of the

By the NUMBERS 13—the number of errors committed by Brooklyn fielders in losing the 1916 World Series to Babe Ruth's Boston Red Sox. Shortstop Ivy Olson made four errors while Ruth and his mates yelled, "Hit it to Ivy."

DID YOU KNOW . . . That Brooklyn pitcher Leon Cadore shared a feat with Boston Braves pitcher Joe Oeschger that will never be duplicated? They both went the distance in a 1–1, 26-inning tie at Braves Field, each throwing more than 300 pitches. Cadore slept for 36 straight hours after the game. Both pitched within a week of their marathon performances.

highest-paid players in the game with a five-year, $9,000-per-year contract, batted .316. Left fielder Zack Wheat batted .312. Pitcher Jeff Pfeffer was a star with a 25–11 record and 1.92 earned-run average. Larry Cheney won 18 and also recorded a 1.92 ERA. Former A's pitching sensation Jack Coombs came over and won 13 games.

The end of the 1916 season was marked by gambling accusations against John McGraw. They turned out to be unfounded, but gambling was a major problem in baseball. Hal Chase of the New York Yankees was said to regularly bet on, and throw, games. It would all come home to roost three years later when the infamous "Black Sox" scandal hit.

The 1916 World Series was a big disappointment for Brooklyn. Babe Ruth and the Red Sox outclassed them. Brooklyn committed 13 errors in the five-game loss. In light of what we now know, one finds this suspicious.

Boston was the defending world champion. Manager Bill Corrigan's crew was 91–63 despite the sale of the great Tris Speaker to Cleveland. They were a fundamentally sound team—baseball royalty—in the middle of a stretch in which they won four World Series between 1912 and 1918 (then waited until 2004 to repeat the act).

The Red Sox were intertwined with Boston's Irish political aristocracy. John F. Kennedy's grandfather, known as "Honey Fitz," was the mayor of Boston. He rode his popularity in conjunction with the winning team, appearing at games, throwing out ceremonial first balls.

Boston's fans, known as the "Royal Rooters," serenaded opponents with songs meant to unnerve them, often achieving that result. Twenty-one-year-old Babe Ruth was the best pitcher in baseball, a 23-game winner with a 1.75 ERA. Robinson, in response to Boston's lineup consisting of four left-handed hitters, inexplicably sat ace pitchers Jeff Pfeffer (just three innings in relief), and Larry Cheney (until the final game), with disastrous results in the four-games-to-one loss.

The Lost Season

In 1920, Brooklyn, still known as the Robins in many baseball circles, won their second National League championship (of the modern era). However, in accordance with what would be viewed as their star-crossed history over the years on the East Coast, the season—and all their accomplishments—were totally overshadowed by events off the field or in another New York borough.

Even their efforts in the 1920 World Series loss to Cleveland are marred by the fact that in that Series the Dodgers managed to be the only team victimized by a triple-play in the fall classic.

Casey Stengel was no longer a Dodger (or Robin), but he remained a fan favorite even when he returned to the stadium with Pittsburgh. In 1919 at Ebbets Field he misplayed a fly ball, incurring some gentle razzing. Noticing that Brooklyn pitcher Leon Cadore had captured a sparrow in the dugout, Stengel retrieved the bird from Cadore, placing it under his cap. When he stepped into the batter's box that inning, amid good-natured hooting and hollering, Casey removed the cap, from whence the sparrow flew out. Stengel bowed amid great laughter and applause.

Stengel later starred for the New York Giants' champions of 1921–22, and became the Dodger manager after Wilbert Robinson retired. Eventually, of course, he made his great name with the Yankees of the 1950s.

America entered World War I in 1917. Many ball players served. Giant great Christy Mathewson was the casualty of a mustard gas accident. He fell sick, never recovered, and died tragically young a few years later. The Americans finally pushed the Germans out of the entrenched Argonne Forest in the fall of 1918, giving the Allies victory.

IF ONLY . . . Hall of Fame pitcher Rube Marquard had not been arrested by Cleveland police for scalping tickets to his Game 4 start versus the Indians in the 1920 World Series, manager Wilbert Robinson would not have started Leon Cadore instead, disrupting the rotation and leading to four straight Tribe victories.

Sports took on greater meaning in America in the succeeding years. College football became wildly popular. Babe Ruth would revolutionize baseball, but in the immediate postwar years a sickness hung over the game like a death knell.

The sickness came in the form of gambling. It was an open secret that baseball was crooked, although other sports were not immune. Even Notre Dame's All-American football star, George Gipp, was said to have been in cahoots with gamblers in 1920 when he sat out a big game. His decision to come back and play the last meaningless minutes, despite nursing pneumonia, was possibly done to mollify critics or assuage his guilt over the incident. Either way, the pneumonia worsened and he died.

In 1919 the Chicago White Sox lost in ignominious fashion to the underdog Cincinnati Reds. Critics suspected the Series was fixed but had little proof. Accusations flew. In 1920 the "Chicago Eight," led by the legendary outfielder "Shoeless Joe" Jackson, were tried for the crime of throwing the World Series.

They were acquitted. The ruling came down toward the end of the 1920 season, in which the White Sox were in first place and expected to avenge their Series loss in a few weeks. Instead, new baseball commissioner Judge Kenesaw Mountain Landis suspended all eight players for life, beginning immediately.

The suspension hit baseball like a ton of bricks. Without their stars, the White Sox lost their lead in the closing weeks of the 1920 season to Tris Speaker's Cleveland Indians, but all the attention was focused on the "Black Sox" scandal.

In the National League, Brooklyn's 93–61 record was an afterthought. The only on-field news that anybody paid attention to was not in Flatbush, but in the Bronx. In an effort to revive interest in the game in the wake of the 1919 Series, the powers that be decided to liven up the baseball. The old, mushy baseballs of the "dead-ball era" were replaced by tightly wound, hard spheres. Furthermore, it was decided that new, shiny white baseballs would be incorporated into play regularly, instead of playing with dark, scruffy balls often retrieved from the stands after foul hits.

Lastly, "outlaw" pitches such as the spitball, emory ball, nick ball, licorice ball, and other "tricks" of the game's early days, were outlawed. A handful of pitchers who specialized in these trick pitches were identified and allowed to use them in their repertoire until retirement.

Burleigh Grimes was the last legal spitballer. Photo courtesy of Getty Images.

One of these pitchers was Burleigh Grimes of the Dodgers who, able to continue plying his trade, was 23–11 with a 2.22 earned-run average in 1920. Grimes would be the last spitballer to finally retire (although many would argue that Don Drysdale and Gaylord Perry carried on his "tradition").

The decision to give an advantage to the hitters was made in large part because Babe Ruth was traded by Boston to the New York Yankees prior to the 1920 season. Ruth, baseball's best pitcher, had in 1919 become an offensive power, slamming 29 homers with the dead ball amid great excitement. Boston owner Harry Frazee traded him to New York in order to finance a Broadway play called *No, No, Nanette,* which nobody ever confused with *Othello.*

It was the beginning of the so-called "Curse of the Bambino." Boston, baseball's best team, went 86 years between world championships. New York was the epicenter of commerce, entertainment, and sports; a symbol of American strength after winning World War I. Plans were in the works to build Yankee Stadium for Ruth.

In 1920 Ruth hit an astounding 54 home runs, drove in 137, and batted .376. It may have been his best season. Many are surprised to

All–1920s
Dodgers Team

Position	Name
Pitcher	Dazzy Vance
Pitcher	Burleigh Grimes
Pitcher	Leon Cadore
Catcher	Hank DeBerry
First Baseman	Jack Fournier
Second Baseman	Chick Fewster
Third Baseman	Jimmy Johnston
Shortstop	Rabbit Maranville
Outfielder	Zack Wheat
Outfielder	Max Carey
Outfielder	Babe Herman
Manager	Wilbert Robinson

learn the Yankees did not win the pennant that year, finishing three games behind Cleveland, but they won three in a row after that (including the 1923 World Series), dominating the game in the 1920s and 1930s, as well as most decades since.

TRIVIA

How did Floyd Caves Herman get the nickname "Babe"?

Answers to the trivia questions are on pages 178–179

The Yankees became the glamour team of all sports, although John McGraw's Giants managed to beat them in the 1921 and 1922 all–Polo Grounds World Series. As for poor Brooklyn, Ruth and the "Black Sox" scandal reduced their 1920 pennant to the background.

Robinson's team did it with pitching and little else. Wheat, the only legitimate star, hit .328. Grimes led the staff, followed by Cadore with 15 wins, Pfeffer with 16, and the still-effective Marquard with 10.

The World Series was a best-five-of-nine affair for a number of years, and Cleveland took the 1920 classic five games to two. Player-manager Tris Speaker led Cleveland. One of the all-time greats, Speaker seemed to age 25 years over a decade. By 1920 the "Gray Eagle" looked like an old man, but he was still a fabulous player, batting .388 and knocking in 107 runs. Pitcher Jim Bagby was 31–12, the next-to-last American Leaguer to win 30 until Denny McLain in 1968.

The Series was unmemorable except for Game 5. With Cleveland winning 7–0 in the fifth, Brooklyn had two men on base (Pete Kilduff and Otto Miller) with nobody out. Pitcher Clarence Mitchell smoked a line drive to the right side. Both runners were off with the hit. Cleveland second baseman Bill Wambsganss made a leaping grab. He ran to second, doubling up Kilduff. Miller ran right into him and was tagged out to complete the triple play. It is the only triple play in Series history, but even more unusual, it was an unassisted one.

The "Daffiness Boys"

The period between 1921 and 1941 is a very important part of Dodger history for various reasons. During this period the Dodgers cultivated a certain kind of "lovable bum" image that was similar to the "Cubbie" image in Chicago; friendly, entertaining, funny losers. But to Brooklynites, the Dodgers were *their* losers. Also established during this time, despite the best efforts of the Giants, was the Dodger-Giant rivalry.

Columnist Westbrook Pegler pinned the nickname "Daffiness Boys" on the Dodgers, but this moniker is slightly misleading. Many attribute it to Floyd "Babe" Herman, an affable hitting star of the era whose poor fielding and base running was as laughable as the heir apparent to the "Daffiness Boys," the 1962 Mets.

It is also tied, in the mind's eye, to Stengel (even though he was gone by the time the name was created), whose rubbery facial expressions, even as a young man, were pure comedy. Wilbert Robinson was, like Stengel, too good a baseball man to call a buffoon, but he was portly and semi-comical. The "Daffiness" name seems to hang around his neck.

In truth, the team was given the name early on, in 1923. While it was apropos to "Uncle Robbie," who seemed to get...daffier in his old age, it is as much attributable to pitcher Clarence Vance as anybody else.

Nobody called Vance by his real first name. His nickname was "Dazzy," but there was nothing daffy about his pitching. As great as Sandy Koufax was, it can be argued that from a statistical point of view, Dazzy was as dazzling as the extraordinary Koufax later would be.

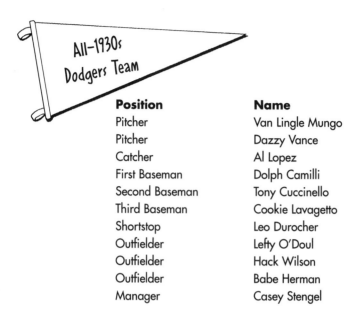

All-1930s
Dodgers Team

Position	Name
Pitcher	Van Lingle Mungo
Pitcher	Dazzy Vance
Catcher	Al Lopez
First Baseman	Dolph Camilli
Second Baseman	Tony Cuccinello
Third Baseman	Cookie Lavagetto
Shortstop	Leo Durocher
Outfielder	Lefty O'Doul
Outfielder	Hack Wilson
Outfielder	Babe Herman
Manager	Casey Stengel

But "Dazzy" and "Daffy" were just too close, and as great as Vance was, the man *looked* daffy. He did not pitch his first full season until he was 31 years of age in 1922, but always looked like an old man. Photos of ballplayers from the early days are simply extraordinary: hollowed faces; ears sticking out like the open car doors; weathered, sunburned, bad skin; haunted eyes. Life was harder. Diets and training regimens were a far cry from today's healthy routines. They drank. They kept late hours but had to play day games on little sleep. Travel was arduous. Hygiene—showers with hot, running water and flush toilets with soft, thick toilet paper—and other amenities like air conditioning, heating, and the like, were nonexistent or hard to attain.

Everybody looked different. It is not an exaggeration to say that when Dazzy Vance was in his thirties, he looked like a man of 55 or 60 in modern America, and this *was* America—the Promised Land, the good life. Americans still looked better and healthier than anybody else did, but venereal disease, polio, Rocky Mountain spotted fever, pneumonia, mumps, and other diseases could still cut a man down.

The "Daffiness Boys" were a team of ruffians not lacking baseball talent, definitely not lacking in personality and color, or what

17

pundits of the era might call "cheek." Nicknames abounded. There were many talented sportswriters in New York, and they handed out sobriquets like "the Four Horsemen of Notre Dame" under a "blue, gray October sky." The Yankees had Ruth (pick your nickname: "Babe," "the Sultan of Swat," "the Bambino") and Lou "the Iron Horse" Gehrig. The Giants' nicknames had gone all the way back to

Dazzy Vance looked like he was 60 years old when he was 30, and by today's standards his pitching motion looked ridiculous. The Hall of Famer's statistics, however, match up with Sandy Koufax's.

Christy "Big Six" Mathewson and "Iron Joe" McGinnity (a Dodger briefly before going to the Giants).

The most common name of the early years was "Rube," including Marquard and later Bressler. Before that there was Rube Waddell of the A's. Long before Chris Berman handed out so many nicknames there was Charles "Casey" (because he was from Kansas City) Stengel, "Uncle Robbie," "Chick" Fewster, "Babe" Herman, "Jigger" Statz, "Watty" Clark, "Sloppy" Thurston (Berman would have called him Howell and figured out how to work "Lovey" in), "Jumbo Jim" Elliott, "Lefty" O'Doul (who should be in the Hall of Fame), "Pea Ridge" Day, "Ownie" Carroll, "Boom" Beck, "Curly" Onis, "Whitey" Ock, Maximillia Carinus ("Max Carey"), "Buzz" Boyle, "Rabbit" Maranville (Hall of Famer), "Snooks" Dowd, and "Frenchy" Bordagaray.

Why not? The alternatives were Hollis, Walter, Manuel, Ralph, William, Raymond, Francis, Harold, Wilson, Clyde, Owen, Arnold, and, of course, Clarence (Dazzy).

"What baseball fan of sound mind and body would choose to root for Hollis and Clyde and Clarence when offered the option of cheering for Sloppy and Pea Ridge and Dazzy?" wrote Glenn Stout in *The Dodgers: 120 Years of Dodgers Baseball*.

All those nicknames, however, could not compare to the one player who had no nickname—talented pitcher Van Lingle Mungo had a lyrical name that inspired jazz ballads. He lasted 11 years, winning 102 games, and was 18–16 in 1934.

Vance was a piece of work, literally. Many players wore white, long-sleeved undershirts underneath their uniform tops, although often the actual uniform was long-sleeved or semi-long-sleeved.

Vance would take the white undershirt and slice it up with scissors. It would hang in strands off his right arm. Robinson often saved him for Monday afternoons at Ebbets Field. Why?

"You might say that the reason I left Cincinnati and went to Brooklyn in the first place was because Vance was there," recalled Rube Bressler in Lawrence Ritter's *The Glory of Their Times*. "If you can't beat 'em, join 'em! Every morning I'd wake up and see him there, and know damn well I didn't have to hit against him that day.

"Vance was by far the toughest guy I ever hit against. Even worse than Walter Johnson. I mean, he was wicked. Oh, he had a curve, it

DID YOU KNOW . . . That Babe Ruth, who was brought in as a Dodger coach (but was just a sideshow in the late 1930s), wanted the managerial job that went to Leo Durocher, who Ruth beat within an inch of his life after Durocher stole his watch when they were Yankee roommates?

started here and broke around your knees, and on account of the contour you couldn't see it. It was like an apple rolling off a crooked table. You couldn't *hit 'im on a Mundy*. On a clear day on a Mundy the batter never had a chance." Bressler pronounced "Monday" *Mundy*.

Vance cut undersleeves, which he whited with lye ("The rest he didn't care how dirty it was," said Bressler). He pitched straight overhand, and between the bleached sleeve waving and sheets of flapping white sheets hanging from clotheslines out of Flatbush apartment houses behind center field, well, "You couldn't *hit 'im on a Mundy*...diapers, undies, sheets flapping on clotheslines—you lost the ball entirely. He threw balls by me I never even saw."

Vance was a true wit, too—a storyteller. He was also part of one of the most famous—and truly "daffy" plays—in Dodger annals. With Babe Herman at bat, Hank DeBerry was on third, Vance on second, and Chick Fewster on first with no outs. Herman hit a ball to right that hit the wall, scoring DeBerry. Vance held up to see if it was caught. He rounded third but was too slow to score, so he headed back to third. Fewster, running head down, arrived at third at the same time. Herman, running fast and not looking, stretched it into a triple. Vance *slid* back into third, where Fewster was standing, just as Herman also slid into the base!

"The third baseman didn't know what to do, so he tagged all three of them," said Bressler. The umpire was confused. An argument ensued among Fewster, Herman, the third baseman, the umpire, the third-base coach, and eventually both managers and the rest of the umpiring crew.

All the while, Dazzy Vance was laying on the ground observing in bemused silence. Finally he lifted up his head and stated, like a member of the House of Lords: "Mr. Umpire, Fellow Teammates, and members of the Opposition, if you carefully peruse the rules of Our National Pastime you will find that there is one and only one protagonist in rightful occupation of this hassock—namely yours truly, Arthur C. Vance."

He was right. Fewster and Herman were out. The papers wrote the next day that Babe had "tripled into a double play."

The whole "clown act" of the "Daffiness Boys" may have made for some good laughs, and created an image of lovable boobs, but do not mistake the Brooklyn Dodgers of this era with the "Amazin' Mets" of the 1960s. Brooklyn may not have won any pennants between 1920 and 1941, and sports pages were dominated by the Yankees and Giants, relegating the Dodgers to the inside, or to their provincial *Brooklyn Eagle,* but they had talent. All-time great talent.

Wilbert Robinson, who passed away in 1934, was deemed worthy of the Hall of Fame in 1945. Vance's record: 18–12 (1922); 18–15 (1923); 28–6, league-leading 2.16 ERA (1924); 22–9, 3.53 ERA (1925); 22–10, league-leading 2.09 ERA (1928); and 17–15, league-leading 2.61 ERA (1929). He was elected to Cooperstown in 1955.

Babe Herman played for Brooklyn from 1926 to 1931, then finished up with the Dodgers after six years with the Hollywood Stars of the Pacific Coast League. He finished with a .324 lifetime batting average.

Casey Stengel returned to manage the Dodgers in 1934–35. He did not win, but he began a lifelong friendship with a young rookie. Raoul "Rod" Dedeaux came out of Hollywood High School in Los Angeles and the University of Southern California, where he was a star player. Dedeaux made the briefest of brief major league appearances under Stengel's tutelage. After he took over as USC's coach and Stengel became the manager of the Yankees, the tradition of big-league teams playing spring training exhibitions against college clubs began. The Yankees, in the days before the Dodgers moved to the West Coast, would barnstorm to L.A. in order to showcase themselves to the nation, playing Dedeaux's national champion Trojans. When Stengel retired, he became Dedeaux's Glendale, California, neighbor and a regular at USC's Dedeaux Field.

When Babe Ruth retired from baseball, he wanted badly to become

TRIVIA

When was the first night game played at Ebbets Field?

Answers to the trivia questions are on pages 178–179

TOP 10

Dodgers Hitters

1. Zack Wheat
2. Mike Piazza
3. Duke Snider
4. Roy Campanella
5. Babe Herman
6. Steve Garvey
7. Lefty O'Doul
8. Jackie Robinson
9. Pete Reiser
10. Tommy Davis

a manager. The Dodgers hired him as a coach. He never did manage. In 1934, with Brooklyn mired in mediocrity, the Giants were locked in a struggle with St. Louis for the pennant. They played Brooklyn toward the season's end. Giant manager Bill Terry was asked about the importance of the Dodger series.

"Is Brooklyn still in the league?" he snorted.

Terry's remarks incensed the Dodgers and their fans, spurring Brooklyn to an upset over New York, helping the Cardinals win the championship. The true nature of the Dodger-Giant rivalry marks its beginnings to this event.

A Whole New Ballgame

What goes around comes around. Things move in cycles. Choose the cliché, but eventually there is truth to it. In the case of the Yankees, well, maybe not. They dominated the 1940s just as they did the 1920s and 1930s. But the 1940s saw a paradigm shift in the fortunes of National League baseball in New York.

What happened? Quite simply, the Dodgers became truly competent, from top to bottom. Sharp executives in the front office; savvy managers in the dugout; stars on the field; and an innovative farm system.

John McGraw finally retired as manager of the Giants. They managed to defeat Washington in the 1933 World Series, but they were soundly beaten by the Yankee juggernaut, led by young Joe DiMaggio, in the 1936 and '37 Series by a combined eight games to three.

After that, the Giants went on a downward slide while Brooklyn improved. The turning point in the entire history of the Dodger franchise can be marked to the memorable 1941 season, which many consider the best year in the game's history. With war ravaging Europe, prior to Pearl Harbor, DiMaggio had a 56-game hitting streak. Ted Williams homered to win an exciting All-Star Game and finished with a .406 average—the last of the .400 hitters.

It started when Larry MacPhail was brought in. Charles Ebbets and his partner, Ed McKeever, died within a week of each other in 1925. Steve McKeever feuded with Wilbert Robinson and, like other "gentleman owners" such as Tom Yawkey, ran the team more like a family charity than a business.

National League president Ford Frick was concerned with his league during the Great Depression. The key to success was New

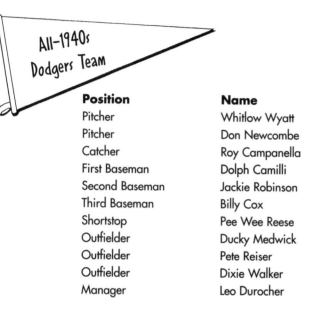

All-1940s Dodgers Team

Position	Name
Pitcher	Whitlow Wyatt
Pitcher	Don Newcombe
Catcher	Roy Campanella
First Baseman	Dolph Camilli
Second Baseman	Jackie Robinson
Third Baseman	Billy Cox
Shortstop	Pee Wee Reese
Outfielder	Ducky Medwick
Outfielder	Pete Reiser
Outfielder	Dixie Walker
Manager	Leo Durocher

York City, but the Giants were descending and the Dodgers were small-time. Frick insisted that MacPhail be brought in. MacPhail was in it to win and make money—bottom line. Ironically, McKeever died shortly after MacPhail's hiring, leaving "executive vice president" MacPhail in complete control.

He was an Army officer who, after World War I, came close to capturing Germany's Kaiser Wilhelm and bringing him to justice, but fame eluded him when the Kaiser barely did. MacPhail was educated and successful in business. He brought those skills to baseball. In St. Louis, he handled the finances while Branch Rickey built the Cardinals into a powerhouse. The team made a profit, drew huge crowds despite the times, and built baseball's first real farm system.

MacPhail moved on to Cincinnati, where he turned that moribund franchise around, brought in night baseball, and then in a drunken rage knocked out owner Powell Crosby!

This made him available. Brooklyn brought him in and gave him unlimited powers, like Napoleon in France or Julius Caesar in Rome. MacPhail radically changed the game and the team. He poured improvements into Ebbets Field, installed lights, and put the Dodgers in the spotlight when they played a night game in 1938. Cincinnati's Johnny Vander Meer threw his second straight no-hit game that evening, a feat never repeated. He designed the uniform style that exists to this day.

Interest in the team increased. The "daffiness" image was replaced by a wonderful cartoon caricature of a "Bum" by Willard Mullin of the *New York World-Telegram.* The team first began to broadcast home games (and away games by re-creation) on the radio. Red Barber was hired and was a hit.

MacPhail brought in players who could take advantage of the short right-field fence. He brought in Babe Ruth as a "celebrity coach." Ruth thought he was a shoo-in to be named manager after Burleigh Grimes was fired, but MacPhail was not going to entrust his team to the wild-living Babe.

The biggest and best move MacPhail made was to hire Leo Durocher, a shortstop who had played for the Yankees and the Cardinals' famed "Gashouse Gang," to manage the team.

It was a successful, but not harmonious, relationship. Both MacPhail and Durocher were headstrong, combative, and liked to drink. But it worked. In 1939 they drew nearly a million fans and turned a $100,000 profit. MacPhail "fired" Durocher over super-prospect Pete Reiser. Reiser was one of the great players ever, his career later cut short by injury. Rickey signed him for the Cardinals. Judge Landis did not like the Cardinals' farm system, declaring it a monopoly. Rickey arranged to trade Reiser to Brooklyn, whereby his

How good was Pete Reiser? Leo Durocher, who managed both men, said Reiser was "better than [Willie] Mays." Injuries prevented Reiser from reaching his full potential.

By the NUMBERS

.343—"Pistol Pete" Reiser's 1941 batting average, when the second-year superstar center fielder led Brooklyn to the pennant along with a .558 slugging percentage, plus a league-high 39 doubles and 17 triples. He led the NL in stolen bases in each of his next two seasons, but a fractured skull derailed his meteoric career.

protégé MacPhail would "hide" him in the minors until he was ready for the big leagues, then trade him back.

Durocher, unaware of the arrangement, brought Reiser up and refused to sit him down or trade him. The press called him "Pistol Pete." No longer "hidden," Reiser had to be played and MacPhail was unable to fulfill his promise to Rickey. He was a superstar until he banged into the outfield wall one too many times, sustaining injuries that reduced him from great to good.

Durocher was "hired" back. A combination of old and young players turned Brooklyn into the 1941 National League champions. Ducky Medwick, the 1937 Triple Crown winner at St. Louis, was signed. Pee Wee Reese was brought in to play shortstop.

The pennant race was a donnybrook with St. Louis. The lead changed hands 10 times. Durocher endeared himself to Brooklyn's feisty, frantic fans with extended arguments with umpires. His pitchers engaged in dangerous "beanball wars." Outfielder Dixie Walker was dubbed the "People's Cherce" in Brooklyn-speak. Reiser hit a league-best .343. Dolph Camilli slammed 34 homers over the "tailor made" right-field fence.

When Brooklyn captured the flag, 60,000 people paraded from the Grand Army Plaza through Brooklyn. Unbelievably, they became more popular than the lordly Yankees, demonstrating the power of the "underdog" or "little guy" in an America that fell in love with Frank Capra movies of the same theme.

Martin Kane of the *Eagle* wrote that the Dodgers were now a "fad with New York's swank international set which hangs out at *Fefe's Monte Carlo* and the *Colony*." Mayor Fiorello LaGuardia pledged his support to the Dodgers, as did singer Kate Smith.

The Brooklyn Dodgers had arrived.

Then the Roof Fell In

The Yankees are the baseball version of America: so much bigger, better, richer, and more successful than anyone else that their excellence, while admired and often loved, seems at times to be overwhelming. Man's natural tendency toward jealousy and covetousness will always produce detractors of the Yankees and the United States, none of which stops both of them from winning and succeeding at virtually all things they engage in, whether it be World Series or wars. The Yankees are the baseball version of Sherman's march to the sea; Patton on his way to Berlin...not always pretty, and a lot of destruction left in their wake.

Yankee history does not include any "Merkle Boners" or "Snodgrass Muffs." Their highlight tapes do not include any pinstriped Bill Buckners letting easy grounders under his glove, or Yankee fans interfering with key pop flies, as in the Steve Bartman incident at Wrigley Field in 2003.

This being the 21st century, hindsight tells us that Brooklyn finally won the 1955 World Series. As if to exorcise any remaining demons, the Los Angeles franchise won three in their first eight years. But until these events came to fruition, before the "Curse of the Bambino," the long droughts of the Cubs, the Red Sox, and White Sox, before any of the other tales of long-suffering fandom, the Brooklyn Dodgers were the kings of disappointment.

It starts with 1941. Before 1941, they were just happy to be there. After 1941 they had to live with the most perilous "close but no cigar" scenarios conceivable, most of them suffered at the hands of rival New York teams.

The 1941 Brooklyn Dodgers entered the fall classic as the "mouse that roared," but as the great writer Ring Lardner once said, "I am not superstitious, but I do think it is bad luck to bet against the Yankees." He was right. It was not even close.

Durocher made the bad decision of holding out 22-game winner Kirby Higbe. Brooklyn might have made a Series of it but for a play in Game 4 that seemed to embody the "wait till next year" mentality of Dodgers baseball in the pre–West Coast days.

Trailing two games to one, the Bums had a chance to tie it up at two. Trailing 3–0, they put on a rally to take a 4–3 lead. Enter Hugh Casey; Southern-born pitcher, reputed spitball artist. Casey clung tenuously to the one-run lead until the ninth. The tension at Ebbets Field was unbearable. Without TV, fans clung to Red Barber's radio description. As any true sports fan can tell you, the radio is tough on the nerves.

TRIVIA

In Game 3 of the 1941 World Series, Brooklyn's pitcher versus the Yankees was until then the oldest ever to start a World Series game. Who was it?

Answers to the trivia questions are on pages 178–179

Ninth inning, Brooklyn's finest lining the field to prevent wild fans from storming the field. *The Dodgers are beating the Yankees!*

Johnny Sturm. *Yer outta here.* Red Rolfe. *See ya.* Tommy Henrich...

Henrich: a clutch hitter; not DiMaggio, but a star player; a mainstay of the Yankee dynasty. Money. But Casey worked the left-handed hitter to a two-strike count, then let one fly that fooled *everybody.* Henrich, completely bamboozled, took a half-swing.

"It was a bad pitch—I mean a ball—but it had me completely fooled," he said in Glenn Stout's *The Dodgers: 120 Years of Dodgers Baseball.* Henrich's failure to check his swing caused umpire Larry Goetz of the National League to raise his hand and call out, "Strike three," as in "Yer out!"

But...

The pitch just as completely fooled poor Mickey Owen, the catcher. Many said it was a spitball gone haywire, although Owen insisted it was a curve and the fault was his; he failed to drop to his

In a seminal moment, catcher Mickey Owen lets strike three get away from him. Tommy Henrich reached first, Hugh Casey could not get anyone else out, and the Yankees rallied to beat Brooklyn in Game Four of the 1941 World Series, thus ushering in a period of disappointment in Dodger annals.

knees to keep it in front of him. The baseball skidded toward the Dodger dugout and a scene of chaos ensued. Only in Brooklyn.

The Dodger players began to head in, arms raised in celebration, if only for a moment.

The police immediately rushed the field to provide a cordon that would dissuade the crazies from rushing the green plains as New Yorkers later did when the Mets and Yankees won championships in the 1960s and '70s.

TOP 10

All-Time Botched Plays

1. The "Merkle Boner," when Fred Merkle's failure to touch second cost the Giants the 1908 pennant.
2. Mickey Owen's passed ball in the 1941 World Series cost the Dodgers Game 4.
3. The "Snodgrass Muff," when Fred Snodgrass's drop of a pop fly cost the Giants the 1912 World Series.
4. Bill Buckner's failure to field an easy grounder that cost the Red Sox the 1986 World Series.
5. Bill Buckner's "first out at third base," when he failed to stretch a single and error into three bases, costing the Dodgers a chance to tie Game 5 of the 1974 World Series.
6. Bill Russell's "dropped liner" and throw that hit Reggie Jackson's hip, costing the Dodgers Game 4 of the 1978 World Series.
7. Babe Ruth's failed stolen base attempt to end the 1926 World Series.
8. The "Lindstrom pebble," a grounder that took a bad bounce, depriving the Giants of the 1924 World Series.
9. Mike Andrews's two errors, costing Oakland Game 2 of the 1973 World Series.
10. The Dodgers' running into a triple play in the 1920 World Series.

Henrich, dejected, stopped the morbid walk back to the dugout—and the clubhouse—when he saw the baseball rolling under the cops' feet. The best description of all came from the *New York Herald-Tribune*, which said that Owen went after the ball "in a vivid imitation of a man changing a tire, grabbing monkey wrenches, screwdrivers, inner tubes, and a jack, and he couldn't find any of them."

Owen had to "thread his way through the police," according to Stout. Henrich made it to first base. Next up: Joe DiMaggio. The fact that DiMaggio would make a hit was well known by every patron of Ebbets Field prior to his accomplishing the act. The Dodger faithful just sat there and watched the "roof fall in," according to sports-writer Tommy Holmes. It did not matter that Casey got two strikes on DiMag. Joe D. hit in 56 straight games that summer, most seemingly with two strikes. He singled.

It did not matter that Casey got two strikes on the powerful "King Kong" Keller. Form played out perfectly when Keller doubled to drive in both runs and put New York ahead, 5–4. It should have ended then and there, so demoralizing was it to endure, so "excruciating to recount," wrote Stout.

As if to assure no hope would remain in order to create further opportunity for agony, the Dodger defense suddenly became a sieve, and it was 7–4 (after the four-run inning) when the Dogs went down like the French army in the bottom of the ninth.

"I lost a lot of ballgames in some funny ways," drawled Casey, whose name at least is memorialized forever, "but this is the first time I ever lost by striking out a man."

The "only in Brooklyn" theme was echoed by the *Herald-Tribune*'s Red Smith, who wrote, "Nowhere else in this broad, untidy universe, not in Bedlam or in Babel nor in the remotest psychopathic ward nor the sleaziest padded cell...could a man win a World Series game by striking out."

Casey has been portrayed as a sympathetic character, in that he induced the third strike only to be betrayed by Owen's failure to block it, he *still* failed on two-strike counts to DiMaggio and Keller, and *did* fail to close the door, instead allowing the mighty Yankees to bust it wide open.

"When you give the Yankees a reprieve," moaned one Brooklyn rooter, "they leap right out of the chair and electrocute the warden."

The rest of the Series is too desultory to Dodger sensibilities to recount in detail. New York finished it off at Ebbets without ever going back to Yankee Stadium, winning four games to one.

A few months later, the Japanese bombed Pearl Harbor. President Franklin Roosevelt announced that, for the morale of the country, baseball would be played, but for the most part players under the age of 30 would be subject to the draft. In 1942, the war effort was in its infancy and many men, including ballplayers, were not yet off to war, but there was a strong sense that the team needed

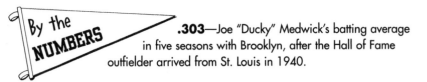

.303—Joe "Ducky" Medwick's batting average in five seasons with Brooklyn, after the Hall of Fame outfielder arrived from St. Louis in 1940.

to "win it now." Players would be lost to the service, never to return, lest they grow too old—or worse!

Reiser was hitting .380 in July of 1942. He collected 19 hits in 21 at-bats. Durocher, not given to hyperbole (he was a man who played with Babe Ruth and later managed Willie Mays), once stated unequivocally that Reiser was "better than Mays."

The implications of just how good Reiser was are lost to the modern fan. Whether he was better than Mays, well, just the possibility that he was is all that need be said. But he was always hurt—beanings, collisions, freak plays. In 1942 he fractured his skull almost making a spectacular catch versus St. Louis. He played again but, like Tony Conigliaro years later, suffered from blurred vision. Despite the bad eyesight he was a valuable player for years, but never achieved the records he would have. It is not inconceivable to believe that he would have been a player in Stan Musial's class or better, and that the Dodgers of the early 1940s would have won the pennants and World Series titles that Musial's Cardinals won.

"He That Will Not Reason Is a Bigot"

In 1967 *Sports Illustrated* published a glorious coffee table book of photos and text from its then-13-year-old magazine called *The Wonderful World of Sport*. The best chapter was "The Characters." The most telling, rare color photo of all was of Branch Rickey.

Rickey, dressed in a tweed suit with bow tie, displays the stern visage of a Wesleyan preacher. He holds a baseball, stands next to an open Bible, and behind him is a framed verse that tells all that need be known about Rickey and his ultimate place in baseball history: "He that will not reason is a bigot; he that cannot reason is a fool; and he that dares not reason is a slave."

To understand Branch Rickey is to understand baseball and its interchangeable coexistence with America, politics, race, and competition. Rickey brought in Jackie Robinson, thus breaking the color barrier. The story is a complicated one. Rickey's Christian faith was the driving force behind his actions. Others worked to integrate sports—like Bear Bryant's integration of Alabama football after losing to Southern California in 1970 or Don Haskins's starting five black players against an all-white Kentucky team en route to the 1966 NCAA basketball championship. Rickey, however, was motivated by winning, by money, and the accoutrements that come with it.

Rickey was highly unusual in baseball. Born in 1881 in Lucasville, Ohio, he played 119 major league games as a mediocre catcher with a .239 batting average. He befriended Cornelius "Connie Mack" McGillicuddy, the legendary manager of the Philadelphia A's. They were kindred spirits; both soft-spoken Christian gentlemen in a game of roughnecks.

Very few baseball players were educated beyond the one-room schoolhouses of the American prairie or, if they lived in a city, high school. Rickey earned a Bachelor of Literature from Ohio Wesleyan University in 1904; a second degree two years later; a law degree from the University of Michigan in 1911; and an advanced law degree from McKendree College in 1928.

Rickey might have been a country lawyer. He might have been a college professor. He might have gone into politics, or he might have gone into the seminary. But he was a baseball man, one of the first to apply the talents of academia with the values of Christianity to the making of successful baseball clubs. Rickey coached at the University of Michigan. His star player was George Sisler. He then managed Sisler with the St. Louis Browns, a poor ballclub, but Sisler was one of the game's all-time legends, a .400 hitter.

Rickey was an innovator who understood the bottom line. He took over the moribund St. Louis Cardinals. Turning that franchise around, he developed the Cardinal image, built the fan base, made key trades and, most importantly, started the game's first farm system.

The understated Rickey's association with the wild and wooly "Gashouse Gang" of Pepper Martin, Leo Durocher, and Dizzy Dean is one of the game's unique turns of fate, but Rickey knew when to "live and let live."

When World War II began, Larry MacPhail was filled with *wanderlust.* The man who wanted to "kidnap the Kaiser" in 1918 saw himself as indispensable to the war effort. "Wild Bill" Donovan's OSS, the precursor of the CIA, was recruiting bright lawyers and intellectuals to form the backbone of a spy agency bent on destroying Nazi Germany and Imperial Japan. MacPhail wanted in. He quit baseball in pursuit of that. There is no record that he ever entered the inner circles of America's intelligence pantheon, but his patriotism in offering his services is admirable.

With MacPhail gone, Rickey decided to take the Dodger offer to replace him. He immediately set his sights on breaking the color barrier. The Brooklyn connection is absolutely critical to this process. Rickey would have run into stiff opposition in St. Louis, which is almost a Southern state; the great "Missouri compromise" before the Civil War revealed strong pro-slavery sentiment there. But Rickey saw in Brooklyn a melting pot of religions and ethnicities. If it could be done, Brooklyn was the ideal place.

In fact, according to Harvey Frommer's *Rickey and Robinson,* one of the club's owners, George McLaughlin, was very interested in signing a black player. Rickey outlined plans to sign a harvest of young Dodgers, forming a farm system better than his St. Louis organization.

The times were tough, with war raging, but Rickey understood the American character. "For the Japanese, to die is to be glorified," he said. "To live hopefully and joyfully is the American objective, and our fighting must match the religious frenzy of the [Japanese] who die."

Rickey saw the war as a battle between the forces of good and evil, with America undoubtedly fighting for good—and God. For this reason he broke his lifelong ban on personal attendance at Sunday

Leo Durocher (left) and Branch Rickey were a true "odd couple." Durocher was a carouser and a womanizer. Rickey was a devout Christian teetotaler. Nevertheless, they made Brooklyn a success in the 1940s.

TOP 10

Sports Events in Civil Rights History

1. Jackie Robinson breaks into the big leagues with the Dodgers in 1947.
2. Jesse Owens wins multiple gold medals in front of Adolph Hitler in the Berlin Olympics, 1936.
3. Sam "Bam" Cunningham's integrated USC football team beats Bear Bryant's all-white Alabama Crimson Tide in Birmingham, 1970.
4. Joe Louis beats Max Schmeling for the heavyweight boxing title in 1936.
5. Texas Western's all-black starting five beats all-white Kentucky to win the 1966 NCAA basketball championship.
6. Black running back C.R. Roberts runs for 251 yards in the first half to lead integrated USC over all-white Texas at Austin, 1956.
7. Black boxer Jack Johnson wins the heavyweight championship in 1910.
8. The Cleveland Indians sign Larry Doby and Satchel Paige, who help them to the 1948 World Series.
9. Negro League All-Stars barnstorm in Latin America, 1930s.
10. USC-UCLA football games feature integrated teams (including Jackie Robinson) in front of mammoth crowds at the L.A. Coliseum in the 1930s.

games to make a pregame speech promoting war bonds before a Dodgers-Phillies game, leaving the park afterward.

The discovery of Robinson was very much a part of the well-oiled Brooklyn scouting machinery. He was a talented ball player, found and signed the same way as the other talented stars, like Duke Snider from California, who would form the great Dodger teams of the late 1940s and 1950s.

Rickey understood that if he could pull off the successful integration of Major League Baseball, his name would resound throughout history. Because the cause was noble in the Christian sense to him, this was well worth pursuing and dealing with the inevitable brick-brats.

It is also very important to note, as Glenn Stout aptly does in *The Dodgers: 120 Years of Dodgers Baseball*, that many—white and black—worked for the change. Rickey has been praised as the paternal white savior, but he was shrewd, and sometimes all things to all people.

He was "a player, manager, executive, lawyer, preacher, horse-trader, spellbinder, innovator, husband and father, politician, logician, obscurantist, reformer, financier, sociologist, crusader, sharper, father-confessor, checker shark, friend, [and] fighter," wrote Red Smith. His nicknames reflected the contrarian nature of the "all-purpose" Rickey: "the Mahatma" and "el Cheapo."

While he had told McLaughlin that he planned to scout the Negro Leagues, this was not made public early on. The scouting of Robinson was done in secret. It worked because many things were happening at just the right time.

The Negro Leagues were filled with talented players, many of whom were well known by white fans who saw them match big leaguers even-up in exhibitions. Brooklyn was by now a totally integrated society. World War II had matched the "everyman" American against the racist, Aryan "superman" of Adolph Hitler's deranged ideology. What were we fighting for? Blacks were fighting in the war, too. Were they to be denied their full rights upon their return?

He that will not reason is a bigot; he that cannot reason is a fool; and he that dares not reason is a slave.

The war also provided a little-recognized opportunity. So many young players were in the service that Rickey was almost forced to look to the Negro Leagues for talent; established talent, too.

The civil rights movement, black society, and the political factions surrounding it were not ignorant to Rickey's intentions, even if he was doing it in secret. Rumors of the Jim Crow baseball law's abolition had abounded for years, but picked up now because the war changed perceptions. Rickey's views were public.

The American Communist Party, which was at its greatest strength because the Soviet Union was an ally during the war, tried

TRIVIA

While Jackie Robinson is well known as a Southern Californian— raised in Pasadena and an athlete at UCLA—he was not born in Los Angeles. What is his birthplace?

Answers to the trivia questions are on pages 178–179

to attach itself to the issue for years. They were strongest in New York, where for various reasons they were made attractive to some of the borough's large Jewish population.

Rickey's staunch conservatism and Christian faith helped stanch the "Communist conspiracy" theories leveled on the "Negro rumor" situation. Again, the issue was not all about morality. Dollars and sense—the American capitalist system—weighed in. New York was one of the only places in America where blacks had some political power in the 1940s. With that came economic power. Many blacks had good jobs and could afford to attend games. They made up a huge percentage of the Ebbets Field gate. The business side of baseball was far from the last thing on Rickey's mind.

He was elected to the Hall of Fame in 1967, and frankly—sadly— he would have made it to Cooperstown even if he had been a racist, based on his success as a general manager in St. Louis and Brooklyn and his role in creating the farm system. But in the end, Rickey's morality is rightly what stands out in the minds of most historians charged with analyzing his place in the game.

Mr. Robinson

Many sports legends do not hold up under scrutiny. Babe Ruth was a reprobate. Ty Cobb was despised. Joe DiMaggio was a self-indulgent egomaniac. Away from the field of play, Barry Bonds is the epitome of unimpressive.

Jackie Robinson holds up. Yes, he got bitter at the end. He made some intemperate remarks and riled some folks, but Robinson was the real deal. And Rickey deserves a great deal of credit because he chose Robinson after a long process in which, as they said in the space program, "many are called, few are chosen." Robinson truly had "the right stuff."

Robinson was not the best baseball player in the Negro Leagues. Satchel Paige, Josh Gibson, and "Cool Papa" Bell were just a few of the more famous stars, but they were aging or gone by the mid-1940s. Paige might have succeeded in the role because of his engaging personality, but he also would have been made the butt of jokes—his down-home homilies were used to belittle the intelligence of the black mind. Buck O'Neil was a good ballplayer, but his lack of education would have been used against him for the same reason as Paige. Gibson was a drunk and a drug abuser. He died young, and it would have been a disaster if he had brought all his problems into the big leagues.

Robinson was the perfect choice. There were few, if any, who had such a background, who presented such a complete and appealing package. Willie Mays and Henry Aaron, who came along just a few years later, had the talent but were naïve youths who might have been broken by the kind of pressure Robinson endured early on. They both have acknowledged as much while paying homage to Robinson.

Even Robinson's black teammates—Don Newcombe, Roy Campanella, and Joe Black—rode on Robinson's back, protected by his out-front position, shielded by his willingness and ability to deflect the "slings and arrows of outrageous fortune" in this most Shakespearean of Brooklyn fables. Robinson was a real-life *Othello*, *Hamlet*, and *Macbeth* rolled into one 5'11", 225-pound bundle of explosive energy.

Start with his athletic ability. Robinson was one of the greatest baseball players of all time, one of the finest second basemen to play the game, the 1947 Rookie of the Year, an MVP (1949), a perennial All-Star (1949–54), a world champion (1955), and a Hall of Famer (1962).

Baseball, however, was his *fourth* best sport. In assessing the greatest all-around athletes ever, Robinson's name must be mentioned with Bo Jackson, Deion Sanders, and other multisport stars. He grew up in Pasadena, California, an L.A. suburb ironically known for its patrician white affluence. Robinson and his talented older brother, Mack, starred at Muir High and at Pasadena City College on integrated teams.

Robinson was All-City in baseball, basketball, football, track, and, just to top it off, was Los Angeles City *tennis champion*. This was not the tennis champion of Yuma, Arizona. This was golden L.A., home of the rich, the famous, and the private tennis court. Players like Bobby Riggs and Jack Kramer had come off the courts of L.A.

Robinson was better at football and track than baseball. He was arguably as good in basketball. At UCLA he crowded all these sports into his busy schedule, but had to give up on tennis, lest he beat the pants off the swanky rich kids swatting for the Bruins.

Playing for UCLA's baseball team, however, Robinson was *terrible*. Maybe he was too tired and too taxed to take regular batting practice or concentrate on the game.

If Robinson had never played professional sports, he still would have been a very big deal in college football. In Southern California, USC

TRIVIA

On December 13, 1956, Jackie Robinson was traded to the New York Giants. What did Brooklyn get in return?

Answers to the trivia questions are on pages 178–179

All-Time
Dodgers Team

Position	Name
Right-Handed Pitcher	Don Drysdale
Right-Handed Pitcher	Dazzy Vance
Right-Handed Pitcher	Orel Hershiser
Left-Handed Pitcher	Sandy Koufax
Left-Handed Pitcher	Don Sutton
Relief Pitcher	Eric Gagne
Catcher	Mike Piazza
Catcher	Roy Campanella
First Baseman	Steve Garvey
Second Baseman	Jackie Robinson
Third Baseman	Ron Cey
Shortstp	Pee Wee Reese
Outfielder	Zack Wheat
Outfielder	Duke Snider
Outfielder	Babe Herman
Manager	Walt Alston

was the dominant program; UCLA was an afterthought. But Robinson and another black star, Kenny Washington, spurred the Bruins to two remarkable ties against USC at the L.A. Coliseum, which turned the game into the fierce rivalry it is today, elevating UCLA into the pantheon of college football powerhouses. Robinson was a national figure who averaged 13 yards a carry in 1938.

Furthermore, the USC-UCLA rivalry played a major role in the development of civil rights. On the West Coast, integration was common in high schools and colleges. USC's first All-American, Brice Taylor in 1925, was black. Dr. Ralph Bunche was a black UCLA basketball star who went on to win the Nobel Peace Prize for his efforts at brokering a Mideast peace accord.

Integrated Trojan and Bruin squads doing battle in front of upwards of 100,000 fans on the Coliseum turf, with their exploits described by radio to wide audiences and written about in metropolitan dailies with large circulations, had the enormous effect of making integration look commonplace, thus making whites accepting of it in California. The fact that the team of Robinson returned to the town of Robinson, even if they did so without him on the roster any more, was most appropriate.

It is also extremely important to note the dynamic of Robinson growing up in an integrated environment, with white friends, teammates, classmates, teachers, and fans. A Southern black thrust into an environment of white people might have been intimidated, whereas Robinson was comfortable.

Fate played a role in Robinson's future in several ways. First, World War II canceled the 1940 Olympics. Instead of dedicating himself to the Games, Robinson had to find an alternative for his sporting energies. There was no money to be made in track, anyway. He was better in football, but football was just as white, with little in the way of an alternative "Negro football league" to pay the bills (although he did moonlight on a semi-pro team).

Jackie Robinson (here stealing home in a 1948 game with the Boston Braves) may have been the most exciting player in baseball history.

Basketball was also all-white. There were the Harlem Globetrotters and little else. But baseball offered the black player a chance to play a joyful game and make a decent living. The Negro Leagues were tough; hot, lots of travel, doubleheaders, even triple-headers on dusty fields. They played year-round because the pay was not enough to take the winter off. So their winters were spent in the warm-weather states or even Latin America, which is why baseball is popular there today. Blacks had a hard time finding meaningful non-baseball work, anyway. It was not the major leagues, but aside from Hollywood, the jazz scene, or international music, it was the best life for most black Americans.

Jackie Robinson had a college education from one of the finest universities in the land. Many college-educated blacks were reduced to menial jobs—porters, waiters, maître d's. But Robinson had name recognition. Had he chosen to go into the professions, he very likely could have forged a fine career for himself in law, business, and very possibly politics. Another black athlete from UCLA named Tom Bradley went into the police force and later was elected mayor of L.A.

But Robinson was an athlete. The competitive fires that drive athletes are impossible to put out, and Jack Roosevelt Robinson was as competitive a man as ever lived. Oh, he was competitive! The problem was that Robinson had gotten just two hits in his last 60 at-bats at UCLA. This is an inexplicable fact of his life. He was not new to the game, having played it at Muir and starred as a shortstop at Pasadena City College.

Despite this, the black press was already pushing Robinson as the "black messiah" to integrate baseball. Looking back, it would seem he would have been chosen to integrate the National Football League (a couple of blacks had played in the 1920s, but no doors had subsequently opened). After all, the high-profile colleges featured integration, but the fixation was on baseball.

All the talk of Robinson and the color barrier seemed to have no real meaning when the United States entered World War II. Robinson joined the army and became a commissioned officer, a feat in and of itself. An incident in Texas was telling, however.

Dressed in a full officer's uniform with rank insignia, Robinson got on a public bus and was told to sit in the back. He decided to take

By the NUMBERS 9—the number of black National League Most Valuable Players between 1947 (when Robinson broke into the league) and 1960. They include (with Dodgers in bold) **Robinson (1949), Roy Campanella (1951, 1953, 1955),** Willie Mays (1954), **Don Newcombe (1956)**, Hank Aaron (1957), and Ernie Banks (1958–59). There were no black American League MVPs until Elston Howard of the Yankees (1963).

a stand. This was not the custom in California, where he was cheered by huge throngs at the Coliseum. He was serving his country, preparing to fight for freedom. Robinson was arrested and charged. He fought the case and won. It was later made into a movie called *The Trial of Jackie Robinson.*

Robinson never went into the combat theatre. He had honed his baseball skills in a semi-pro league at Brookside Park, located adjacent to the famed Rose Bowl. In the army, he played on service teams, which were very competitive during the war, what with so many players drafted. Given an honorable discharge, he went into the Negro Leagues. He was considered a "college boy" by the grizzled vets. He struggled at times. It was a tough league, pitchers with lots of tricks up their sleeves, a hard game to succeed at. There were better players than Robinson, but his background, which may have created a little jealousy, immediately made him the subject of talk that maybe, if the "right kind" of guy could make the move, he was it. When Robinson found his groove, he managed to hit .387, which, considering that he batted a pathetic .097 at UCLA, is a testament to his prowess as an athlete.

Branch Rickey's scouts immediately spotted him. Robinson was not the only one. Rickey knew that a plethora of major league–caliber baseball players—potential stars, greats of the game—toiled in those leagues. Some were young men who could contribute to the Brooklyn Dodgers for years to come. This was a fabulous chance to turn Brooklyn into a dynasty. It had to be done carefully, with kid gloves. The Roy Campanellas, the Don Newcombes, the Larry Dobys; all were like ripe fruit waiting to be plucked from the tree.

But one man had to open the door so the rest could follow. One extraordinary man. Rickey decided that man was Jackie Robinson.

"I Want a Player with the Guts *Not* to Fight Back!"

Judge Kenesaw Mountain Landis, who had upheld the "gentleman's agreement" barring blacks from baseball, died in 1944. There was no rule, no law prohibiting blacks. There was only the will, the courage—or lack thereof—to do the act.

Rickey had been scouting Robinson in secret, but it was too big to keep under wraps. The rumors flew like crazy. The war in Germany ended in May 1945; in Japan a few months later. In 1946 baseball had a new beginning.

Freed from the draft or back from the service, 400 new prospects were signed by Rickey. They were assigned to spots in the vast Dodger farm system. His scouting of Negro League players was as extensive off the field as on. He had private detectives dig up every bit of personal information possible about black baseball stars: education, family, religion, criminal records, whether they had white friends, marriages, abortions, gambling habits, everything.

Many excellent players were scratched from the list because they did not meet Rickey's stringent moral code, but Rickey knew how important it was that these first black players be able to withstand white scrutiny. The tiniest flaws would be magnified.

Robinson's trial for not taking a seat in the back of the bus in Texas was interesting to Rickey. He did not want a militant, but he did want somebody capable of standing up for himself. Transcripts of the trial indicated that Robinson stood proud in a tough situation.

The external factors were all there. Robinson was a great all-around athlete who could play all four infield positions—second base, shortstop, first base, or third base—if need be. He could run

TOP 10

All-Time Greatest African American Players

1. Willie Mays
2. Barry Bonds
3. Hank Aaron
4. Frank Robinson (Dodgers)
5. Josh Gibson
6. Satchel Paige
7. Roy Campanella (Dodgers)
8. Bob Gibson
9. Jackie Robinson (Dodgers)
10. Reggie Jackson

like the wind, steal bases (an art that had been lost since Babe Ruth revolutionized the game with homers), hit for average and for power.

Rickey loved the fact that Jackie was a college man. His California background worked in his favor, too. First, Robinson had grown up in an integrated society. Second, Rickey's scouts were scouring the West Coast, always a hotbed of talent, and now, amidst the beginnings of the postwar Baby Boom, a growing populace of athletes. These were not Southern or Midwest whites with ingrained prejudices, but a new breed of man who Rickey knew to be tolerant.

Then there was Robinson himself. He was movie-star handsome with a winning smile. His voice had no rural twang or street lingo to it. He spoke the King's English with perfect locution, the essence of a well-educated man, almost like the California beach accent attributed to a later generation. Then there was Robinson's wife, Rachel, who was nothing less than adorable. They were *perfect.*

There was just one last issue that needed to be resolved. That was Robinson's fiery, competitive nature. The very thing that made him so great—the toughness honed on the gridiron during his college days, the willingness to absorb and *deal out* physical punishment—concerned Rickey.

Robinson, who fought for his rights, would fight for his honor. He was proud, and he was going to have his pride tested. Horrible things would be said to him, about him, around him, about his family, by fans, by opponents, by the press, by *teammates.*

Scout Clyde Sukeforth gave Robinson one last look-see. He was 26, a tad old in Rickey's estimation, but the maturity might prove helpful. One final check was made to ensure Rickey of the man's moral uprightness, and after that it was "all systems go."

Sukeforth asked Robinson to accompany him to the Dodger offices under the ruse that Rickey wished to sign him for a team called the Brooklyn Black Dodgers, who played at Ebbets Field when the big leaguers were on the road.

The two met. Robinson, a smart cookie, knew this was the moment. He was not here to play for the *Black* Dodgers. Rickey tested the man, using language and describing behavior that was completely out of his usual character. Rickey role-played race-baiting players, fans, and umpires. Robinson listened, polite but

Jackie Robinson, the big-league's first black player, reports to spring training in Sanford, Florida, in 1946. He is greeted by Branch Rickey's assistant, Robert Finch.

puzzled. In a famous exchange, Robinson quizzically asked, "Mr. Rickey, do you want a player who is afraid to fight back?"

Robinson was a fighter, and not just in the metaphorical sense. He knew how to use his fists and was prepared to do just that in Brooklyn.

"I want a player with the guts *not* to fight back!" Rickey said.

"I get it," he said. "I've got another cheek."

Robinson was signed for a $3,500 bonus and a $600 per month contract. The black press reported the rumor that Robinson was signed for 1946, but the white media steered clear of it. When the formal announcement was made on October 23, 1945, the news shocked America.

The Brooklyn that Jackie Robinson entered was a new and improved Brooklyn. The Naval Shipyards provided employment for tens of thousands. Service members passed through town, many taking in games at Ebbets Field. Betty Smith's 1943 novel *A Tree Grows in Brooklyn* was a national best seller.

But it was not Brooklyn at first for Robinson. It was Montreal. As in Canada. The Dodgers had purchased a franchise in Montreal, called the Royals, which was the perfect place for Robinson to make his debut in organized professional baseball, not to mention open the baseball market to Canada.

But before Montreal there was spring training in Florida, which is of course the South. The Dodgers trained in Daytona; the minor leaguers 30 miles away in Sanford. This was not the Florida of modern-day Miami: a melting pot of anti-Communist exiles from Fidel Castro's Cuba. This was the Jim Crow South.

Sanford literally kicked the Dodger minor leaguers out of town because of Robinson, forcing them to relocate to the black section of Daytona. The pressure was already intense, and the focus was on Robinson. He made it through that, then mercifully left for Montreal.

At Montreal, the manager was a Mississippian named Clay Hopper, who had no love for Robinson.

TRIVIA

What did Yankee rookie catcher Yogi Berra say that fired up Jackie Robinson prior to the 1947 World Series?

Answers to the trivia questions are on pages 178–179

DID YOU KNOW . . . That Cookie Lavagetto, who broke up Bill Bevens's no-hitter in the 1947 World Series, had been a Dodger regular before the war, but when he came back Branch Rickey told him he was through and should take a managing job in the low minors? Lavagetto refused to quit, and his name is now enshrined in Dodger lore.

Robinson started slowly, but picked up his game. He was the talk of baseball, his outstanding play making it obvious that it was only a matter of time before he would be in Brooklyn...and then what?

Oddly, the Dodgers blew the 1946 pennant, in a roundabout way, because of Robinson. Locked in a tight struggle with St. Louis, they badly needed to bring Robinson up from Montreal. There was no question that he could propel the team. Leo Durocher, considered an amoral man of little character to speak of (a true contrast with Rickey), nevertheless possessed one appealing trait, which was a seeming lack of racial prejudice. He just wanted to win and did not care who or what helped him do the winning. He lobbied for Robinson.

But Rickey had a timetable. To bring Robinson up in 1946 would upset the apple cart, and he decided against it. Robinson was the premiere minor league baseball player of 1946, leading Montreal to the Little World Series championship with a .349 batting average.

In Brooklyn, the Dodgers were edged out by St. Louis, who gained ultimate glory by beating Ted Williams and the powerful Boston Red Sox in a seven-game World Series. But that was the end for the Redbirds. They would not field a champion again until 1964. They had no black stars of note while successful teams in both leagues did. Then under new ownership and—irony of ironies—under the guidance of Rickey, brought in as an "advisor to the president" in 1963, they formed a team of proud, educated blacks, Latinos, and Southern whites. They would form what writer David Halberstam deemed to be the baseball version of the 1960s Democratic Party, defeating the baseball version of the pinstriped GOP, the Yankees, in the Series.

But Jackie Robinson's ascendancy to Brooklyn would usher in the greatest era in Dodger history, in New York history, and probably in baseball history.

The Good Samaritan

Walter O'Malley lived by the law of the jungle. He is a hero in L.A. because his selfish decisions benefited his new city, but O'Malley reminds one of a famous quote by a wise man who said, "What you do is so loud I cannot hear what you say."

So it was that O'Malley could make fun of Rickey, who was never part of baseball's hard drinking "boys club," but stands above almost all of them because, as President Andrew Jackson once said, "One man with courage makes a majority." Rickey and Robinson alone constituted a true American majority.

O'Malley bought out Rickey, denying him the kind of wealth that could have been his had he been allowed to share in the eventual "California Gold Rush." Robinson died frustrated, but to the lover of Truth and Justice, the winners in the end are Rickey and Robinson, not Walter O'Malley.

Rickey was set in his ways. He did not drink and avoided those who did, which was not easy in baseball. Larry MacPhail drank. Leo Durocher drank. Walter O'Malley drank. But when Rickey's daughter was married, he served no alcohol. He advised his guests that if they desired a drink, there was a bar down the street.

O'Malley was schooled in the corrupt Tammany Hall–type culture of New York's political machine, updated to the 1940s and '50s. He felt that his methods were of no concern to Rickey. Rickey dressed like a rube, with a bow tie and a suit befitting a preacher—in rural Ohio.

But aside from the differences between the two men, Rickey had the upper hand when it came to the most important aspect of their shared business, which was baseball. He was a former major league catcher with years of experience as a college coach, big-league manager, and successful general manager. By the time O'Malley made his appearance on the scene, Rickey had already established his *bona fides*.

It was also Rickey who created the famed "Dodger way," which became popularized by later sermons from Tommy Lasorda and a book by Al Campanis. At a time in which training and coaching methods were haphazard, Rickey developed a franchise mentality, teaching young players how to slide, catch, play the field, and throw strikes. It allowed coaches and managers throughout the organization to teach in a uniform method. As players moved up the ladder, they were not constantly exposed to new, confusing philosophies. It was the baseball version of McDonald's.

To the extent that Walter O'Malley, who had some say in the matter, did not block the signing of Jackie Robinson, credit is due O'Malley. But the demographics of postwar America also made it apparent to him that Robinson's signing would be of financial benefit to him.

That said, Rickey was a capitalist, too, who was all about making a profit. He was not above doing so at the expense of his team's comfort, choosing chintzy training quarters and travel accommodations on occasion, or scheduling exhibition matches that did little for the club except increase the bottom line.

Rickey's benevolence has been questioned by some. Rickey claimed that when he was a college coach, he had a black player on his team. When the player was denied a room at a hotel on the road, Rickey said that he went to console him, finding him "scratching his skin off" in a desperate effort to deny his blackness. Rickey stated this was the seed that led him to plan, over the next 30 years, how best to integrate the game he loved.

The player was contacted after the Robinson signing, but said he could not recall the incident in question, although he may have simply wanted to forget about it, which is understandable.

But Don Newcombe was furious at Rickey for not bringing him up in 1948, even though he dominated in the minors and, in a down year for Brooklyn, could have made a huge difference (just as Robinson could have in 1946). Rickey insisted on a "one black player per year" philosophy, which 60-plus years later sounds a little lame, but considering the temper of the times was a realistic strategy.

The difference between O'Malley and Rickey is that Rickey was a visionary, O'Malley a political opportunist. Thus, it is an irony of

Branch Rickey (right) could get along with most people, including Leo Durocher. Walter O'Malley (left), however, could not take Rickey's righteous ways and "stole" the Brooklyn Dodgers out from under him, thus setting up the move to Los Angeles a few years later.

ironies that O'Malley's move to California is viewed as one of baseball's great visions. Despite all the criticism heaped on O'Malley herein, it was just that. Credit must be given where it is due.

The Rickey-O'Malley partnership lasted six tempestuous years. A breach in the relationship came when O'Malley and another partner opposed the teetotaler Rickey and accepted the sponsorship of Schaefer Beer.

TRIVIA

Of all the baseball scouts Branch Rickey employed to scout the Negro Leagues and other teams looking for the first black player, whose advice did Rickey value the most?

Answers to the trivia questions are on pages 178–179

Rickey also cultivated a business deal with William Zeckendorf, a real estate developer with the vision for a new Dodger stadium, already a pressing issue. The relationship was complicated and ended up costing O'Malley $50,000, which he was determined to make back one way or another.

Rickey was bought out in 1950, replaced by Buzzie Bavasi and Fresco Thompson. O'Malley detested Rickey so much that he "fined" anybody who even mentioned Rickey's name. Bavasi and Thompson never would have gotten the jobs, having worked under Rickey, but they had previously worked under Larry MacPhail, a hard-drinking Irishman of the O'Malley style.

O'Malley just badmouthed the departed Rickey, who left in quiet dignity.

Breaking into
the Big Leagues

Robinson's first year in professional baseball—1946—went well. He played his first game for Montreal at Jersey City, New Jersey, just across the river from Manhattan and Brooklyn. He was received warmly there and, after hitting a home run, was met by a sea of hands by his teammates.

"I wasn't sure if my teammates would shake my hand," he said, breathing a sigh of relief, while also revealing his human frailty, a trait that helped make him a sympathetic figure.

The 1947 season was the most anticipated in baseball history. With the war now two years removed, the economy rolling again, and the United States standing as a powerful nation, there was a sense of triumph, that anything this nation set out to do, it could accomplish. Breaking the color barrier was just another goal that would be accomplished.

This feel-good attitude was not shared by all when it came to the race issue. Indeed, the idea that America was altogether forward-thinking was disproven when, in January, the owners gathered for a secret meeting in New York.

New Commissioner A.B. "Happy" Chandler, a former Kentucky senator, might have been considered hostile to black progress, but to his credit he was a savvy politician who saw the future. But owners like Boston's Tom Yawkey, St. Louis's Sam Breadon, and Philadelphia's Robert Carpenter Jr. did not. Rickey felt his great reputation, forged over the past 44 years in organized baseball, would give him leeway. He was stunned to find staunch opposition. He made it clear that Robinson would play for Brooklyn. His belief in the innate kindness of the human heart caused him to think that the vocal opposition was less bigotry and more for show—until a 15–1 secret vote against Robinson showed him the ugly reality.

Rickey stormed out. The owners thought they had won. Just when Rickey might have felt that evil prevailed, he found light at the end of the tunnel. Rickey was a fighter just like Robinson. He had a few chips to play. First, despite bluster and racism, the majority of this beautiful nation wanted to break the color barrier. Second, the "law" had never been codified, just as "Jim Crow" was, for the most part, not actually in the public record.

Rickey visited Chandler in the bluegrass horse country of Kentucky and was delighted by what the ex-senator told him.

"I'm going to meet my maker someday, and if He asks me why I didn't let this boy play and I say it's because he's black, that might not be a satisfactory answer," he told Rickey. "So bring him in."

Rickey had to sell announcer Red Barber, another Southerner, on announcing Robinson's exploits. The ol' redhead gave virtually the *identical* answer about "meeting my maker" as Chandler had.

In one of the most dishonest photos ever taken, Jackie Robinson and Philadelphia manager Ben Chapman pretend to be friends in 1947. Away from the camera, Chapman's vicious racial remarks cut Robinson to the core.

What Chandler and Rickey counted on was that Yawkey and his breed lacked the courage to fight integration openly and in the public, for all to see. They were masters of the smoke-filled room, the good ol' boys club. Yawkey later rejected *Willie Mays* after a tryout in 1950. The "curse" of the Red Sox had *nothing* to do with Babe Ruth!

Then came spring training, and with it *utter, total, and absolute confusion!* First, Rickey had the Dodgers and Royals train in Havana, Cuba, while the rest of the organization trained normally in Florida. The idea was that Robinson (as well as Roy Campanella and other blacks signed over the winter) would face less racism. Rickey also figured the white Dodgers would get used to the sight of black faces in Cuba. But Rickey also figured the Cubans would fill the stands for exhibition games. Making money was part of the motivation. The Dodgers stayed at a spartan military academy, which also saved money, but Robinson was housed miles away in poor conditions with the other blacks, for reasons that have never really been explained.

The Dodgers had plenty of Southerners on the team, including the aptly named Dixie Walker of Georgia, Kirby Higbe of South Carolina, Pee Wee Reese of Kentucky, and Eddie Stanky of Alabama (a second baseman defending his position). A revolt was orchestrated by Walker, resulting in a petition, trade demands, and other pleasantries, but Durocher put it down.

Spring training was more of a circus than a camp. Rickey counted on Robinson's talents shining through, thus demonstrating his value to his teammates, who in turn would want him on board. It did not work out that way. He became an ostracized figure. Then Robinson injured his back.

As if that was not enough, Durocher, whose iron hand and take-charge leadership style was badly needed, first had to leave for California, where the divorce status of his wife, actress Laraine Day, was challenged. Then Chandler suspended him for one year because of his open association with gamblers.

History has never shed true light on the suspension. Some speculate that Durocher was suspended to create big news, taking the hot glare of public attention off of Robinson. Others have said Durocher really did not want Robinson, because Eddie Stanky was his "kind of player." Others thought that Durocher and Rickey were incompatible, and Rickey wanted him out (although the timing is too poor to justify that). Others said Larry MacPhail was behind it, for nebulous reasons.

Clyde Sukeforth was made interim manager. Robinson officially made the club, which had not been a sure thing amid the craziness. He would play first base. Stanky, a valuable player, remained at second. Robinson played in an exhibition series versus the Yankees.

An extremely important point was made when large crowds, including many blacks, showed up and cheered Robinson. Walker, the former "People's Cherce," was booed.

On Opening Day, a strangely subdued crowd of 26,623 turned out. Robinson went hitless, handled his first base duties well enough, and the team won, 5–3. Vendors hawked "I'm for Jackie" buttons. Walker's supporters made their presence known this time, cheering Dixie, but Jackie was received politely.

The season began to play out and nerves were rattled. The team had been forced to make changes and deal with the extraordinary events: the strange spring training, the Durocher suspension, the rumors and tension. It was extremely hard for Robinson, but it was difficult for his teammates, too, no matter what side of the fence they stood on (in truth, many straddled that fence). As if there was not enough turmoil, Sukeforth was replaced by Burt Shotton.

Robinson played well at the Polo Grounds against the Giants, and things were looking pretty good, but all hell broke loose when Philadelphia came to town, led by their anti-Semitic, racist Southern manager, Ben Chapman.

For three games, the entire Phillie team unloaded verbal assaults

TRIVIA

What was Branch Rickey's favorite expression?

Answers to the trivia questions are on pages 178–179

$100,000—the amount of money earned by Jackie Robinson in the winter of 1947–48 for endorsements, speaking engagements, and signing to star in a movie of his life. He reported to spring training in 1948 badly out of shape.

on poor Robinson that were as "bad as anything you can imagine," recalled Howie Schultz. "If they said those things today it would cause a civil war."

It was abominable, yet oddly it worked to Robinson's advantage. Brooklyn fans heard it and felt badly for the quiet man standing at first base. His teammates took Robinson's side. Stanky, who had the most reason to dislike Robinson, told the Phillies to "pick on somebody who can answer back."

Rickey made the bizarre proposition that Philadelphia move their home games to Ebbets Field for the remainder of 1947. His motivation was to make money, to draw fans who were both for and against Robinson, but also it may have been, as Michael Corleone said in *The Godfather: Part II,* to "keep your friends close, but your enemies closer." The Phillies declined.

The season played out, mostly not according to plan. The Cardinals tried to strike instead of playing against Robinson. The FBI investigated death threats and police inspected rooftops for snipers. Several racist Dodgers who were expendable were traded or sent to Montreal. Slowly, Robinson's teammates gained respect for him. Ever so slowly, he began to play better and better. The team, wallowing around the .500 mark, finally made their move, although when Pete Reiser was badly hurt again, crashing into the concrete outfield wall at Ebbets Field, it was a major blow.

The press arranged for a photo of Chapman and Robinson shaking hands, which in light of Chapman's actions is repulsive to look at. Dodger attendance did not pick up as much as Rickey liked. White fans stayed away, either because they did not like Robinson or did not like the increase in black fans at Ebbets Field. Attendance throughout the league, however, picked up as the curious came out.

The turning point came when Robinson faced a particularly hostile crowd in Cincinnati. The Kentuckian Reese walked over to him, putting his arm around his teammate. Tears flowed from the compassionate. Reese and Robinson forged true friendship. Truth and beauty slowly but surely overtook hatred and bigotry, just as Branch Rickey faithfully thought it would.

By midseason, Robinson was hitting .310 and Brooklyn led the league by a game. Cleveland owner Bill Veeck, seeing "the Experiment" working, brought Larry Doby, the first black player in the American League, to Cleveland. The horse was out of the barn.

"Wait Till Next Year"

In 1941, when Brooklyn lost in five games to the Yankees after Mickey Owen's strike three/passed ball, Dodger fans consoled themselves with the fact that they had at least *made it* to "the Big Dance."

But after that, there was little consolation. From 1942–46, the Dodgers lost a series of close pennant races with one of their rivals, St. Louis. While the Giants continued to be—and are to this day—their major rival, the Cardinals are a very close second, often more competitive. The all-time series record between the two clubs goes back more than 100 years, but stays around the .500 mark.

A strange, nagging feeling was beginning to gnaw at Dodger fans; the idea that the team was not destined for ultimate greatness. Pete Reiser's constant flow of serious injuries, which interrupted a career so brilliant as to be beyond the ability to speculate, helped fuel this fire. Could it be that Brooklyn was just too small-time to enjoy the fruits of a world championship?

Many thought that the signing of Jackie Robinson had put the Dodgers squarely on the right side of history and that the baseball gods would reward them with a world title.

Spurred by Robinson, the National League's Rookie of the Year and a .297 hitter in 1947, Brooklyn soared to the National League title with five games to spare (94–60). Robinson's treatment was still abysmal in many quarters, but it improved markedly, especially with his teammates. Grudging respect made way for admiration at his dogged determination, his intelligence, his ability to withstand pressure, and, of course, for his marvelous skills as a batsman, glove master, and especially his base-running acumen.

TOP 10

All-Time Greatest Catchers

1. Josh Gibson
2. Ivan Rodriguez
3. Johnny Bench
4. Mickey Cochrane
5. Roy Campanella (Dodgers)
6. Yogi Berra
7. Mike Piazza (Dodgers)
8. Bill Dickey
9. Ernie Lombardi
10. Thurman Munson

Robinson revolutionized the game. His aggressive, take-no-prisoners style was the beginning of what would come to be called "National League baseball." It would make the senior circuit the better league over the next 25 years. Unfortunately, it did not make them the better team. That was, and would continue to be, the New York Yankees.

By season's end, nobody could deny that "the Experiment" had succeeded. Doby was making his mark in Cleveland, and when Rickey brought in another black, Dan Bankhead—whose good work gave the team much-needed pitching down the stretch—that just cemented the deal.

The 1947 World Series was one of the most memorable ever played. Cookie Lavagetto of Brooklyn broke up a ninth inning no-hitter (with two outs) by New York's Bill Bevens to win Game 4, 3–2.

With an 8–5 lead in the sixth inning of Game 6, Brooklyn left fielder Al Gionfriddo robbed Joe DiMaggio of a two-out home run. Footage of DiMaggio kicking the dirt after the spectacular grab is legendary, as is Red Barber's memorable call and his signature "Whoa, doctor!"

Robinson ran *wild* against the Yankees. He got into rundowns, stole freely off the great Yogi Berra, and taunted the Bronx Bombers. But in the end, Brooklyn ran out of pitching while the Yanks had plenty. In the seventh game, Robinson went 0-for-4, marking the Dodgers' doom. New York won, 5–2. Brooklyn fans just had to say, "Wait till next year."

In October 1947, while the Dodgers were losing to the Yankees, an event was taking place in the skies above California's high desert that would have a major effect on the team. Chuck Yeager, a "natural-born hero" from West Virginia, broke the sound barrier in a test flight out of Edwards Air Force Base, about an hour from Los Angeles.

News of the event quickly spread. The United States had perfected jet flight, something the Germans and Americans had fought to make happen first, in peacetime. That meant coast-to-coast air travel and with it, eventually, expansion. Tommy Holmes wrote an article shortly thereafter detailing Happy Chandler's plans to do just that.

Robinson opened the door for other African American players, like pitcher Don Bankhead (with manager Burt Shotton).

By the NUMBERS

16—The age of Tommy Brown, the youngest Dodger ever, who also became the youngest to hit a home run, at age 17.

In 1948, despite being the defending champions and introducing Robinson into the major leagues, the Dodgers' attendance sagged. In a three-team market, they were third. It was obvious that Ebbets Field was not accommodating to the modern, big business of baseball.

Spring training was again a haphazard affair. Robinson strangely came in overweight and did not play himself into shape until well into the season, which, in retrospect, seems almost impossible to believe. But apparently he was giving himself a break after the rigors of 1947.

Rickey made the curious choice of barnstorming the Dodgers through the South. It was financially lucrative, and perhaps satisfied Rickey's "in your face" desire to make integration's success plainly obvious to Dixie, but it was not kind for Robinson. Maybe Rickey thought more had changed in 1947 than really had.

Leo Durocher was eligible to come back, but Rickey did not want him. Their personalities were too different, but "Leo the Lip" was popular so Rickey needed to play along. He signed him but forced him out at midseason.

Stanky was "traded" to the Boston Braves, but it was really a sale. Many assumed it was because of his views toward Robinson, but Stanky was his biggest supporter by 1948. He immediately made Boston the best team in the National League, who with their "Spahn and Sain and pray for rain" pitching duo of Warren Spahn and Johnny Sain, lost to Cleveland in the World Series. The Indians had just beaten the all-white-and-planning-to-stay-that-way Red Sox in a one-game playoff. Cleveland featured Larry Doby in the outfield and pitcher Satchel Paige, who won many key games down the stretch.

Robinson was moved to second base but was unable to spur the team as he had the previous year. Roy Campanella was brought in to catch. Rickey's policy was one black player per year. Campy was it, but Don Newcombe spent the year at Newark, complaining all the time. Had Newcombe been brought up, they may have beaten the

Braves. Had Rickey signed and used all the black players still available, he would have created a dynasty, but his natural conservatism kept him from turning the team into the "black Dodgers." Rickey told confidantes that he knew the team had to be remade in order to compete beyond 1948. Dixie Walker was let go and a youth movement was started.

Enter Walter O'Malley. O'Malley made a fortune foreclosing on people during the Great Depression. He became the Dodger attorney and parlayed his wealth and influence into part-ownership of the team. He clashed with Rickey, mainly over money. O'Malley felt Rickey spent too much on the farm system.

O'Malley was not satisfied with the rate of his investment return. The problem was Ebbets Field. The city of New York, he reasoned, would have to build a new stadium for his team.

The Old West saw "this town's not big enough for the two of us" applied to Rickey and O'Malley in Brooklyn. O'Malley had the money and was slick enough to grab power from Rickey. Rickey was eventually forced out.

The Lords of Flatbush

In 1949, *finally,* the Dodgers returned to a sense of normalcy in spring training after their ill-conceived Cuban adventure, Southern barnstorming tour, and the hostile environment that Robinson was forced to contend with.

It was arranged for the team to move into an old Navy barracks in Vero Beach, Florida. It was off the beaten path, but this meant fewer Southern racists to heckle Robinson and the growing number of black players. It meant a single "one size fits all" camp for major leaguers and minor leaguers alike; a true "complex" in which the organization could prepare for the season. Over time it would be converted into Dodgertown and is, to this day, the finest spring training facility in the nation.

Jackie Robinson became the best player in the National League, winning the 1949 Most Valuable Player award with a league-leading .342 batting average and 124 runs batted in.

Brooklyn recaptured the pennant from Boston and beat back St. Louis in a tight race. Attendance picked up and they were, for the first time, favored to beat the Yankees in the Series.

In 1949 Joe DiMaggio was old and badly hurt. Out until June with a bad heel, he finally came to play in a key June series at Fenway Park, putting on a legendary performance. Boston was loaded from top to bottom, with the great Ted Williams enjoying one of his finest years. New York's manager was "the clown," Casey Stengel, a move many thought would bring the team down. Instead, he led the club to the league title and would ultimately steer them to their greatest glory, which is saying something!

David Halberstam wrote a book called *Summer of '49*. Between the New York-Boston and Brooklyn-St. Louis pennant races and the Brooklyn-New York World Series, it was quite possibly the best season ever; a year that featured all-time greats, legends at the top of their games, the best towns, most rabid fans, and most successful franchises ever.

For Brooklyn, it was again "wait till next year." They suffered the ignominy of losing to the Bronx Bombers in five games, with the Yankees taking the clincher at Ebbets Field, 10–6.

Despite the success on the field and gate revival, the future was up in the air. Along with jet travel there was suburbanization, highway construction, and car travel. A "white flight" to Long Island and other green pastures occurred. Brooklyn, ironically once considered a suburb, was becoming an "inner city" dominated by blacks and Puerto Ricans. Many Jews moved out, too, with the exception of the Hasidics, who disdained sports for the most part.

TV became commonplace, which meant fans did not have to purchase a ticket in order to watch the games. Games could be heard on the radio while driving, too. O'Malley was complaining to anybody who would listen that he needed a modern stadium with amenities. Every year California and its welcoming arms beckoned more and more.

In 1950 the Brooklyn Dodgers under manager Burt Shotton lost an excruciatingly close pennant race to the hated Phillies. At least Eddie Sawyer had replaced the horrid Ben Chapman, but Jackie Robinson and company saw red—not just Philly's colors—whenever they played them.

By the NUMBERS

$5.35 million—The estimated value of the Brooklyn Dodgers at the time Branch Rickey's interests were bought out by Walter O'Malley in 1950. When Rickey had taken over the club, the team was in debt. When he left, they owned the Montreal ($1 million), Ft. Worth ($400,000), and St. Paul ($350,000) franchises. There were 635 players under contract, dispersed among a farm system of 25 teams, plus 150 in the Armed Forces. Brooklyn had a capital surplus of $100,000 ($900,000 in available cash) and an earned surplus of $2.6 million.

The 1950 Brooklyn-Philadelphia pennant race was one of the fiercest ever. This play, featuring Philadelphia's Dick Sisler breaking up a double play by upending Jackie Robinson, exemplified the action.

Rickey's transformation was complete by 1950. The old guard was replaced by the new. This was the team that would make its name in Brooklyn and echo throughout baseball history. Ironically, it was Rickey's last year. He was bought out and kicked out by O'Malley, who consolidated his financial hold on the franchise while fending off investors who very well may have kept the team in Brooklyn down the road.

At first base was "Gentleman Gil" Hodges (32 homers, 113 RBIs and a .283 average). Robinson (.328) manned second base. The great Pee Wee Reese was a defensive mainstay at shortstop. Billy Cox handled the hot corner. Duke Snider of Compton, California, hit 31 homers, drove in 107, hit .321, and was *the* New York center fielder (Willie Mays and Mickey Mantle were still minor leaguers, and DiMaggio was on his last legs). Hard-edged right fielder Carl Furillo had one of the best rifle arms in baseball and batted .305 with 106 RBIs.

Don Newcombe blazed his way to a 19-win season, as did Preacher Roe, but the rest of the staff was the team's Achilles heel. Ralph Branca was inconsistent and Carl Erskine (7–6) not yet developed. Good pitching beats good hitting, and Philadelphia did just that behind Robin Roberts (20–11), Curt Simmons (17–8), and relief star Jim Konstanty. The reliever was coming into his own. The Yankees' Joe Page had been an integral closer over the past few seasons.

TOP 10

Greatest Pennant Races

1. 1951 Giants-Dodgers
2. 1962 Giants-Dodgers
3. 1967 Red Sox-Tigers-Twins-White Sox
4. 1908 Cubs-Giants
5. 1978 Yankees-Red Sox
6. 1964 Cardinals-Reds-Phillies
7. 1949 Yankees-Red Sox
8. 1950 Phillies-Dodgers
9. 1969 Braves-Giants-Reds-Dodgers
10. 1993 Braves-Giants

With the pennant on the line, Erv Palica defeated Philadelphia in the second-to-last game, meaning the finale would either be a Phillie pennant-clincher or force a playoff. It was the best finish since "officials carried Dorando over the finish line in the 1908 Olympic marathon," wrote Chicago sportswriter Warren Brown, referring to an exhausted Italian who collapsed within the stadium and was dragged—illegally—to the tape.

Having playing four doubleheaders in five days while Philly played three in the same time span, both teams felt like that unfortunate long-distance man of yesteryear, but there were no friendly officials to "carry" them.

The finale was a classic: Don Newcombe versus Robin Roberts, both pitching on fumes going for win number 20. It was 0–0 in the sixth when Philadelphia broke the ice, 1–0.

Then Reese hit a drive into the wire mesh above the left field fence, normally resulting in the ball bouncing back into play. Reese's ball stuck into the mesh, and the umpires ruled it a homer. This was the only time it had happened, but the Phillies "could see that silly little ball stuck in the screen" the remainder of the game, wrote one Philadelphia scribe.

In the ninth, pure luck worked against Brooklyn. The courageous Roberts had runners on first and second. A pickoff play was called. Center fielder Richie Ashburn alertly raced in to back up the pick, but Roberts missed the sign. Duke Snider singled to center. The crowd roared, some even hopping the fence.

Third-base coach Milt Stock did not see Ashburn's head start, racing toward the ball "like a third baseman fielding a bunt," as described by one writer. He waved speeedy Cal Abrams home, but Abrams had hesitated for a split second when shortstop Granny Hamner had moved behind him for the pick that never happened.

Ashburn picked the hop perfectly and threw a strike that nailed Abrams by 15 feet. Robinson, whose faux pas in the sixth had led to the lone Philly run, never had the chance to make up for it. He was walked intentionally. Roberts had nothing left but retired Carl Furillo on a pop-up and gave up a deep drive to left off the bat of Gil Hodges, but Dick Sisler gloved it.

Roberts was not pinch hit for in the tenth. He singled off Newcombe, also going the distance. Eddie Waitkus, best known for being shot by a female "admirer" (an event that became the subject of Bernard Malamud's *The Natural*) singled. Then insult and injury were added to irony when Sisler, the son of Rickey's all-time favorite player—the great George Sisler, who pitched for him at Michigan and played first base for him in St. Louis—homered to send the Brooklynites home for the winter.

DID YOU KNOW . . . That Brooklyn's pitching staff held Hall of Famers Joe DiMaggio and Yogi Berra to a combined 3-for-34 in the 1949 World Series?

The Creeping Terror

David Halberstam makes the case that 1949 was baseball's greatest year. If a thrilling, down-to-the-wire pennant chase in both leagues is his criteria, then so be it. But 1951 may have been more memorable. Not in the American League, where the Red Sox, fully cursed by now after their wholesale refusal to sign Willie Mays because he was black, were dying on the vine. The Yankees won in their usual corporate manner.

But the 1951 National League duel between the Dodgers and Giants may never be matched for intensity of feeling, pressure, thrills, and pure excitement. It is a Giants story, of course, but, alas, no book on Dodger history is complete without retelling the tale in excruciating detail.

It starts with Leo Durocher, given the bum's rush from Brooklyn for various reasons, not least of which was the issue of moral turpitude and whether he had any. The man who judged him unfit, Branch Rickey, was also gone, forced/bought out by Mr. O'Malley much the same way he foreclosed on Depression-era mortgage delinquents.

The Giants were by 1951 the third team in a three-team city by a long shot. Their last pennant was in 1937 with little late-season contention in between. Brooklyn had won three times and had been in it virtually every season since 1941. The Yankees? Think of Napoleon's Italian Campaign, or Teddy Roosevelt's ride up San Juan Hill: brilliant, decisive, victorious.

The Polo Grounds were half-empty. Its Harlem neighborhood was now dangerous. White fans avoided the place, but blacks were for Jackie and the Dodgers, not the Giants. Under Hall of Fame player-turned-manager Mel Ott, the Giants were little more than long-ball artists, knocking 'em out over the short right-field porch, their pitchers and fielders then giving up more runs than they produced. They struck out too much and did not steal bases or go for the extra bag.

Durocher's exile to baseball's Elba was, like the original, short-lived. Horace Stoneham hired him to manage the Giants. Leo brought in Eddie Stanky, a cantankerous Durocher clone who had plenty of motivation to beat Brooklyn.

They signed Monte Irvin, a superb black outfielder. Then they brought up Willie Mays. Suddenly they found themselves playing "National League baseball." Mays was a talent above all others, but he was more than just a five-tool superstar. He was *joie de vivre* and this was what the New York Giants needed more than anything.

The Giants traded spring training sites with the Yankees in 1951. Mays started the season at Minneapolis. By May he was hitting

The Dodgers seemed to have the 1951 pennant wrapped up, until the New York Giants called 20-year-old outfield sensation Willie Mays up from Minneapolis. Here a pensive Mays is shown at the Omaha airport departing for New York and everlasting fame.

about .477. Meanwhile, Durocher's Giants were just plain brutal, while new Dodger manager Chuck Dressen's club was a house afire.

The Dodgers of the 1950s were one of baseball's all-time great clubs, and they knew it. In 1951 they finally were unburdened, or so it seemed, of an intense pennant race with St. Louis or Philadelphia. They looked untouchable. It was not like they had not been there before; they knew they were winners and had the confidence that goes with being champions.

Then Durocher called up Mays. Now, Willie Mays is thought by a lot of people to be baseball's all-time greatest player. It is a tough case to argue against, with the exception of Babe Ruth (only because he was the game's best pitcher before switching to the outfield). As a five-tool guy, though, Mays is nonpareil.

That said, Mays was a rookie in 1951, and his skills were nowhere near what fans saw when he returned from the army in 1954, or his early years in San Francisco. At first he could not hit. He cried to Durocher, begging to be sent back to the minors, but Durocher—and this *was* his greatest moment—assured him he was his guy for defense if nothing else. The story is a well-told one. Mays broke an 0-for-12 start with a homer off Warren Spahn and the rest is history. He hit .274 with 20 homers and 68 RBIs; not Earth-shattering, but in this case the old clichés—*sparkplug, driving force, inspiration*—are as right as rain. At the tired old Polo Grounds, Mays created excitement in the manager, his teammates, the broadcasters, and the fans. Robinson was great; Mays was far better.

Obviously, Willie seems to be the central protagonist, but he could not make pitchers suddenly turn into corner artists, fielders masters of leather, batsmen now seeing baseballs the size of grapefruits. But that is what happened.

It was not so much a Brooklyn folderoo. They tailed off, but by and large the Giants' comeback consisted of winning three out of every four while the Dodgers won three out of every four, then the Giants winning

TRIVIA

When Brooklyn manager Leo Durocher was issued a one-year suspension from baseball for gambling in 1947, what was the official reason offered by Commissioner A.B. "Happy" Chandler?

Answers to the trivia questions are on pages 178–179

IF ONLY ...

Boston owner Tom Yawkey was not dead set against the signing of a black player, Willie Mays (who wowed Red Sox scouts at a tryout) would have been Ted Williams's teammate at Fenway Park instead of signing with the Giants, and surely New York would not have caught Brooklyn for the 1951 pennant.

the next series three of four while Brooklyn split. Brooklyn's 3–1's and 2–2's were always at least matched by New York's 3–1's, with plenty of 4–0 sweeps for good measure. Just like geology, all it took was time and pressure.

Jim Hearn and Sal Maglie were mound maestros. Irvin supplied power. Stanky was a defensive star and on-base demon: hit-by-pitches, walks, scratch singles. Bobby Thomson, often a slump artist, found his groove. Durocher talked his team up, pumping them up to the press and for their benefit. They believed the hype.

But after falling into a deep hole and then making a modest comeback, the Giants again found themselves digging out of a big deficit. On August 8, Brooklyn swept the Giants in a doubleheader, 7–2 and 7–6. Sal Maglie threw one at Robinson's head and a brawl ensued, with the Ebbets Field crowd hurling garbage at Durocher. New York had lost six straight to Brooklyn, who led by 11½.

The Giants could hear through the paper-thin walls Brooklyn's hollering and whoopin' it up in their clubhouse. Dressen told the press, "The Giants is dead." Another story quoted Durocher, apparently inaccurately, that the Giants were done, but he exploded that "I don't give them a thing." With General Douglas MacArthur in the stands, Brooklyn won again, 6–5, making their season record 12–3 versus New York.

On August 11, Brooklyn beat Boston in the first game of a doubleheader to up their lead to 13½. They lost the nightcap to end the day up by 13. They were 70–36; the Giants, 59–51.

Then on August 14, 15, and 16, New York swept Brooklyn three straight. The lead was less than 10. A psychological barrier had been lifted, or imposed, depending on the point of view. The Giants also started stealing signs, courtesy of a system orchestrated between Durocher, his hitters, coaches, and the Polo Grounds scoreboard

By the NUMBERS

72—the percentage of games won by Dodger pitcher Preacher Roe (93–37) in seven seasons with Brooklyn. He also won two of three World Series decisions.

operator. Much has been made of this, with many denials, but the story has never died.

With the Giants suddenly totally on fire, Brooklyn began to suffer small injuries. By early September Brooklyn still led by seven. The "pesky Giants," as the *Brooklyn Daily Eagle* called them, beat the Dodgers twice. Suddenly they resembled the "creeping terror." By September 15 it was five. On September 22 Charlie Dressen's birthday present was an oil painting depicting the Dodgers as "National League Champions of 1951."

Brooklyn lost it: exhausted, slumping, beat up mentally and physically. New York defeated Robin Roberts, and the Dodgers lost a doubleheader to Boston. The lead was now one game, but the advantage was with New York, who had two fewer games to play. Brooklyn needed rest but had none. On September 27 Brooklyn came unglued. Tied 3–3 with the Braves, a close play went against the Dodgers. Their ensuing argument was so vociferous that umpire Frank Dascoli tossed Campanella, Dressen, and the whole bench. Campy was in the clubhouse when his at-bat came around in the ninth. They lost. The lead: half a game.

"The Shot Heard 'Round the World"

Philadelphia beat Carl Erskine, 4–3. Brooklyn and the Giants were now tied in the standings. Newcombe then bested Robin Roberts with a shutout, but Maglie did the same to the Braves. Last day: Larry Jansen beat Boston, 3–2, while Brooklyn fell behind Philadelphia, 6–0. Durocher's team crowded around the radio; at first celebrating, then sweating, then cursing.

Brooklyn, carried by the great Robinson, forged their way back in it. Extra innings, 8–8 with the Giants boarding a train from Boston to New York while announcer Russ Hodges provided play-by-play over a rail phone as they made their way through Connecticut.

All the momentum of an entire season swung in varying ways in this most pressure-packed of games. Newcombe, on no rest, had come on in the sixth and was still valiantly pitching in the twelfth. Bases loaded. Eddie Waitkus hit a line drive to win the game and end Brooklyn's year...except that Robinson "stretched at full length in the insubstantial twilight, the unconquerable doing the impossible," wrote Red Smith. He landed like a football wide receiver, knocking himself woozy, *but did he catch the ball?* That was the $64,000 question.

The umpire checked. *He had!* Robinson could barely walk back to the dugout. The Philadelphia crowd, perhaps his greatest detractors in the early years, gave him a huge ovation. Then he barely made his way back to the bench. Roberts was in.

Did pitchers ever rest in those days?

More zeroes until the fourteenth. Then Robinson smoked a line-drive home run. Philadelphia was held in the unbearable bottom of the fourteenth. The Giants suddenly felt the pressure.

Left fielder Andy Pafko watches in vain as Bobby Thomson's "shot heard 'round the world" lands in the left-field seats.

A playoff, of course. Game 1 at Ebbets Field. Ralph Branca, Brooklyn's best pitcher four years earlier, started. Dressen had lost faith in him, but the staff was depleted. Branca grooved home run pitches to Irvin and Thomson. An injured Campanella could not beat out a double-play grounder in which Snider would have crossed home to tie the game, but no. Jim Hearn bottled up Brooklyn, 3–1.

Game 2, the Polo Grounds. Brooklyn's Clem Labine was superb in a 10–0 shutout.

The decider was at the Polo Grounds on October 3, 1951, a date that will live in infamy for Dodger fans. Campanella was unable to play. Rube Walker would catch, and if he had to be removed, rookie Bill Sharman, who had been called up for the game, would step in.

Preacher Roe was also hurt. Maglie (23–6), exhausted, versus Newcombe (20–8), more exhausted. Maglie was in trouble early but Campanella was not there to knock him out at his most vulnerable.

Brooklyn led, 1–0, but Maglie settled down. Newcombe was throwing seeds, remarkably, as if it was Opening Day. Thomson's base-running blunder spoiled a rally, but in the seventh he hit a sacrifice fly to tie it, 1–1. Newcombe told Dressen to get him out of there, but Robinson got in his face, shaming him into staying in.

In the eighth, Thomson failed to come up with a hard smash by Andy Pafko. Then Billy Cox singled past Thomson, a play he should have made. Brooklyn led 4–1, and it was over.

In the bottom of the ninth, Newcombe trudged out there two innings after he told Dressen to lift him. Alvin Dark, with two strikes, squibbed one between Hodges and Robinson. The "seeing eye" grounder tipped off Gil's glove.

Dear God!

Then Hodges held the unimportant run represented by Dark on first base. Don Mueller hit a double-play grounder to Hodges, except that Hodges was holding Dark, so it went for a single. Runners on first and third, but Irvin popped up for the first out.

Whitey Lockman then inside-outed a double to left, scoring Dark. Mueller sprained his ankle sliding into third. Clint Hartung, once considered one of the greatest prospects of all time (who became one of the biggest busts), replaced Mueller.

Dressen called to the bullpen. For the first time all season, Dressen asked Clyde Sukeforth for his opinion. Labine, coming off a shutout, or the man he did not trust, Branca? Just at that moment Labine bounced a curveball, which was relayed to Dressen, who imagined a wild pitch allowing Hartung to score and the tying run moving to third with one out.

Newcombe left and Branca entered *The Twilight Zone*. Bobby Thomson came to the plate. Willie Mays knelt in the on-deck circle. There were 34,000 people at the Polo Grounds. Millions would later say they were among those 34,000. Ernie Harwell was calling the action on televison and Red Barber and a young Vin Scully were part of the Dodgers' broadcast team. Russ Hodges handled radio chores for New York. The station did not routinely tape games, but a fan in New Jersey was recording Hodges' descriptions.

Pundits have said that the managers decided the game, in that Dressen froze, making a bad call for Branca, and then provided no advice on what to throw. Meanwhile, Durocher may or may not have told Thomson to look for fastballs because he had homered off a Branca slider earlier. Durocher did tell him, "If you ever hit one, hit one now."

Walker, lacking Campanella's experience, decided to jam Thomson up and in with fastballs, but with a 279-foot left-field line Thomson could power one out even if jammed. Newcombe had pitched the Giants' power away all day for that very reason.

Up in the scoreboard, a man may or may not have been relaying signals to Thomson. Thomson says he was not. Others say he was. Branca came in, up and in, but still a high strike was called. Walker had called for two fastballs in the mound conference, possibly to

DID YOU KNOW . . . That Russ Hodges's famed "The Giants win the pennant!" description of the "shot heard 'round the world" was captured by posterity only because a man in New Jersey taped it? In general, radio and TV broadcasts were not preserved. There is no known recording of the televison broadcast, in which Ernie Harwell reportedly said simply, "It's gone."

avoid the scoreboard operator's eye, and also to keep the runner on second from making a signal. But Walker signaled location, up and in again. Branca worked fast, another fastball, fat, up, and in.

Thomson tomahawked it. A fly ball, a liner that started to sink.

TRIVIA

Who was the Dodgers' scapegoat after the disastrous "shot heard 'round the world?"

Answers to the trivia questions are on pages 178–179

"It's gone," said Harwell, thinking of the short porch down the line, but then he noticed it sink and began to change his mind. Andy Pafko waited for it at the 315' sign, but it maintained enough height to breach the fence, which stood 16' high.

Hodges: "There's a long drive... It's gonna be...I believe—*the Giants win the pennant! The Giants win the pennant! The Giants win the pennant! The Giants win the pennant!*"

One of the most famous sports calls in history has been criticized as wildly out of control by none other than Scully, who always tried to stay calm, not be a "homer," and preferred to "let the crowd noise tell the story."

Hodges went on and on, describing the Polo Grounds as "going crazy...whoooooooooo!!!"

Still "Waiting Till Next Year"

The 1952 Dodgers, to their credit, were able to put their '51 memories behind them and capture the National League flag. The Giants, missing Willie Mays (doing a two-year army stretch), were not the same. Brooklyn had their own problems to contend with, namely Newcombe's induction into the service, Preacher Roe's sore arm, and a freak injury to Branca.

O'Malley's penny-pinching ways, however, reduced the farm system and would eventually create an aging ballclub without a strong minor league system to rebuild (if only for a few years). But the Negro Leagues were still a source of talent for Brooklyn, namely in the form of a good right-handed pitcher, Joe Black. The Dodgers used Black mainly out of the bullpen. The role of the relief pitcher was changing. No longer was the bullpen consisting of has-beens, but rather good young arms like Black's.

By July 22 Brooklyn was 60–22, but a replay of 1951 reared its ugly head. They played .500 ball the rest of the way. The Giants rallied again and after sweeping a doubleheader from the Dodgers on September 6 trailed by four.

"If we can pull this out," Leo Durocher said, "there'll be 100,000 suicides in Brooklyn." What a lovely thought from gentle Leo!

Dodger pitching, or the lack thereof, was the problem. But the Giants, lacking Mays and suffering injuries to Monte Irvin and Larry Jansen, did not have it in them this time. Brooklyn prevailed by four and a half games.

O'Malley fumed at the lack of support, however. Only 1 million fans bought tickets. It is a great conundrum of Brooklyn history that the team in its greatest heyday was not well supported at the gate at a time in which the gate was virtually their only source of revenue. Romantics paint the portrait of Brooklyn teeming with rabid Dodger fans. They were loved, yes, but it was always a cult thing. The Los Angeles crowds and popular support overwhelmed the Brooklyn experience.

Crime was a big problem in 1950s Brooklyn, and the *Eagle* did not help its cause by highlighting each heinous act with sensational headlines, thus driving Brooklyn residents—and their subscribers—out of Brooklyn!

Joe Black became the first black pitcher in World Series history when he started Game 1 of the World Series, but his move from the pen to a starter's role was tacit admission by Dressen that he did not have the arms to beat the Yankees. Black won the opener, 4–2. The teams split the first four, but when Erskine won the fifth game it looked like it could be a Dodger year.

Hodges went 0-for-21, Black was beaten twice, and the Yankees won again in a seven-game Series. It was the "coming out" party for Mickey Mantle, a rookie in '51 who finally emerged from Joe DiMaggio's shadow to lead his team to the Promised Land.

In 1953 two rookies, pitcher Johnny Podres and infielder Jim "Junior" Gilliam, made the jump. Gilliam took over at second. Robinson became a utility man, playing third and the outfield.

Republican vice-presidential candidate Richard Nixon shakes Carl Erskine's hand after Erskine's 11-inning, 6–5 win over the Yankees in Game Five of the 1952 World Series.

Campanella was the league's MVP again. He and Snider crushed more than 40 homers each. The Giants slumped and Brooklyn found themselves contending with a young, talented Milwaukee Braves team. A new National League city, Milwaukee's crowds were enormous. The attitude of the baseball establishment, with jet travel now commonplace, was that the future lay out West.

Erskine was the staff ace at 20–6, but Black dropped from his 15–4 rookie campaign of 1952 to a 5.33 ERA. In the World Series with the Yankees, Dressen again showed why he is not considered a good strategist. He pressed the panic button, overusing Erskine (or at least counting on him too much). Campanella suffered a hand injury that curtailed his effectiveness.

Erskine struck out 14 Yankees in Game 3 and Billy Loes won the next day to even the Series at two, but Dressen tinkered with what had gotten them there, using the inexperienced Podres instead of the veteran Russ Meyer in an 11–7 Game 5 defeat. Then Dressen skipped Roe in Game 6. The Yanks won it with a run in the ninth, 4–3, to take the Series.

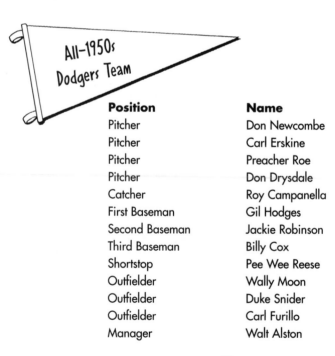

All-1950s
Dodgers Team

Position	Name
Pitcher	Don Newcombe
Pitcher	Carl Erskine
Pitcher	Preacher Roe
Pitcher	Don Drysdale
Catcher	Roy Campanella
First Baseman	Gil Hodges
Second Baseman	Jackie Robinson
Third Baseman	Billy Cox
Shortstop	Pee Wee Reese
Outfielder	Wally Moon
Outfielder	Duke Snider
Outfielder	Carl Furillo
Manager	Walt Alston

By the NUMBERS 15—The major league record for runs scored in a single inning, set by Brooklyn in their 19–1 victory over Cincinnati on May 21, 1952.

"We lost because the Yanks played their usual game in the Series and we didn't," said Reese.

The Dodgers—management and talent—were taking shape for the future. Al Campanis was by this time a scout. Fresco Thompson was the vice president, and Buzzie Bavasi was an assistant. Dressen, who never took any blame, was fired. Walt Alston was hired.

Red Barber and his $60,000 salary were let go, replaced by Vin Scully at $18,000. Sandy Koufax of Brooklyn's Lafayette High School, a freshman basketball player at the University of Cincinnati, was signed. Koufax had been discovered mainly because he found out the Cincinnati baseball team was making an early-season trip to Florida, and he wanted to get some warm weather. Trying out in the Cincinnati gymnasium, his fastball was eye-popping. Campanis found out about him, signing him to a bonus before anybody else could get to him.

With Willie Mays back from the army, the Giants powered their way to the pennant and, to the frustration of Brooklynites, a four-game sweep of Cleveland in the 1954 World Series. Dodger attendance declined again. Fans in New York went for the Yankees and, of course, Willie Mays and the Giants. The automobile was more prevalent than ever. Both the Polo Grounds and Yankee Stadium were conveniently located near freeways. It was problematic at Ebbets, where there was no parking for their increasingly suburbanized fan base.

Milwaukee's County Stadium had acres of parking. The new fans were now typically a family of three or four, packed into the car, leisurely making their way into the park, where they would raid the concession stand. Night games made it easier for schoolkids and working adults to attend weekday games. But nighttime around Bed/Stuy was no place for families by 1954.

For Dodger fans it was just another season of frustration in which the only consolation was to "Wait till next year." Again.

Finally!

The 1955 season is looked back upon as a magical season in Dodger history, but it sure did not look that way at first. Walt Alston was intimidated by the Dodger stars, choosing to communicate with them via the press. He and Jackie Robinson almost came to blows. Alston was accused of racism because the team had five black players and supposedly he was not pleased about that. Alston threatened to bench Robinson, still a star player.

On Opening Day, less than 7,000 fans showed up, but the team was on fire, winning their first 10 games of the season. But fast starts were their forte. So, too, were disappointing finishes.

Pitching was the big difference this time, with Newcombe back in great form. In June, Brooklyn won 16 of 19. Incredibly, attendance dragged throughout the summer. O'Malley fumed. He had the best team in baseball and nobody seemed to care. Radio advertising was the team's best source of revenue, with fans tuning in to Vin Scully, many of them sitting in cars. The idea of millions of Los Angelenos potentially doing the same thing did not escape O'Malley's attention. Westward expansion was more prevalent by 1955. The Philadelphia A's were now in Kansas City. O'Malley made many statements hinting at movement, most of which were ignored: plans to play games in Jersey City in 1956, plans for a new stadium, complaints about "inclement weather," which, of course, meant the whole East Coast. O'Malley courted political figures in order to get a new stadium, to get land, to build parking lots. He also entertained the wholesale interest of other cities in his valued franchise.

On the field, the Dodgers never went into a prolonged slump. On September 8, earlier than any team in National League history, they clinched the title with a 10–2 win over Milwaukee to lift their record to 92–46. The crowd of 300,000 lining the streets to welcome them home from the road trip after the pennant-clincher was three times smaller than that of a few seasons earlier.

The baseball gods, of course, arranged for the sixth Dodger-Yankee World Series. The previous season, Casey Stengel fielded what may have been his very best team, but Cleveland upended them. The Indians needed most of their 111 victories to wrest the pennant from the Bombers. It seemed apropos that in a year the Yanks did not make it to the Big Dance, neither did the Dodgers.

The Yankees were so dominant in the 1950s that rooting for them was like "rooting for U.S. steel," as the saying went. The Mickey Mantle-Yogi Berra-Whitey Ford crew was invincible.

Johnny Podres is mobbed after his 2–0 shutout over New York won the 1955 World Series at Yankee Stadium.

DID YOU KNOW . . . That the 1955 Brooklyn Dodgers were in first place every single day of the season, starting out 10–0, then 22–2, and never relinquishing the top spot?

A popular Broadway play of the 1950s was *Damn Yankees!*— written from the perspective of a Washington Senators fan ("first in war, first in peace, and last in the American League"). The premise of the play was that the only way to beat these guys was to sell one's soul to the devil.

There is no evidence that the '55 Dodgers did that. Alston had managed to lose a pennant race in '54 after Dressen had won two in a row. He was far from popular with anybody, ranging from the players to the press to the fans to the front office, but the fact is that he had the magic touch.

The Yankees, as if they did not have enough advantages, now had added a great black player, Elston Howard, to their lineup. Howard, a catcher, would kick around at different positions until eventually taking over the backstop job from Yogi Berra, but they faced one true difficulty: Mickey Mantle was injured and day-to-day.

New York had the home-field advantage, opening at Yankee Stadium. Newcombe was knocked out and Ford was sailing along, but Jackie Robinson pulled a typical Robinson play when he stole home to make the score 6–5. There was little strategic sense in the play, but it "lit a fire" under the Bums. In fact, replays show that on the razor-thin steal, Robinson may well have been tagged out by Berra, who in a famous bit of footage goes bonkers, jumping up and down to protest the call. When the Yanks took the second game to go up 2–0, it looked bad, but Robinson's steal had put New York on edge.

The deficit had a strange liberating effect. This was a team that had "come from ahead" on several occasions. They knew what it felt like to blow the lead. Nobody expected them to come back in this situation. Red Smith all but wrote them off. But they were in the "business of doing the impossible."

At Ebbets Field, with Mantle healthy enough to hit a homer, Brooklyn blew an early lead and looked to be on the way out. But just when Johnny Podres appeared on the brink of disaster, he recovered to pitch the Dodgers to an 8–3 win. Ebbets Field organist Gladys

Gooding serenaded birthday boy Podres with "Happy Birthday" as he closed it out. (Gooding was a fixture at Ebbets, as was a makeshift band called the "Dodger Sym-Phony.")

On the morning of Game 4, Charles Kiley of the *Herald Tribune* broke a story that Walter O'Malley had commissioned a "geodesic-domed" stadium, apparently in reference to O'Malley's insistence that Dodger fans deserved to be shielded from "inclement weather."

O'Malley was playing various angles against each other. He already had his eye on Los Angeles, but if the city of New York would build him a palace, so be it. But the domed nature of his plans was, a decade before the Astrodome, an object of derision. His real influence came from a later off-season Dodger exhibition of Japan, in which he fell in love with the "field boxes" at a stadium in Tokyo, the below-field-level seats that would later emerge as a distinctive feature of Dodger Stadium.

When Brooklyn won, 8–5, and then again, 5–3, behind Roger Craig, they suddenly were in the familiar, uncomfortable position of frontrunners. Back at the Stadium, their 5–1 defeat had doom written all over it. Podres, talented but inexperienced, was tasked with stopping Mantle and crew at Yankee Stadium in Game 7. The Dodgers were nicked and Alston had to do some lineup shuffling. Robinson's health was a question mark.

October weather in New York is good until midmonth. Today, with extended playoffs, New York postseason games are often played in bitter cold, but Game 7 in 1955 was on a perfect Indian-summer day.

A series of close calls on both sides built the tension until Brooklyn scratched a run in the fourth. Playing small ball, they scored again in the sixth. Then a Cuban-born left fielder named Sandy Amoros entered the game for Brooklyn.

The notorious sunlight peeking over the stands made it difficult to pick up fly balls in left field. Amoros entered the game at the precise time of day and year in which this phenomenon is at its worst. With runners

TRIVIA

In the world championship season of 1955, where did Brooklyn home attendance rank in all of baseball?

Answers to the trivia questions are on pages 178–179

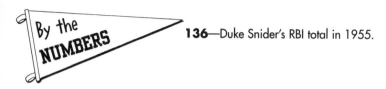

on first and second with no outs, the Dodgers swung everybody to the right against the dead-pull, left-hand-hitting Berra. But Podres and Campanella were determined not to give him a shot at the short right-field porch at Yankee Stadium, as Rube Walker and Ralph Branca had mistakenly done with Bobby Thomson at the Polo Grounds in 1951. Berra saw that he was going to be pitched away and smartly went with it, smacking a hard, twisting, opposite-field drive directly into the setting afternoon sun down the left-field line—*miles,* it seemed, from Sandy Amoros.

Gil McDougald was running like the wind from first base with the tying run, but Billy Martin at second held to see if Amoros could get there. Amoros, the fastest man on the team with Robinson hobbled, ran and ran and ran until he had to brake around the 301' sign, 15 feet from the foul pole. Fenced in by the low railing, the baseball twisting crazily and with plenty of speed, looking like it could clear the fence or bounce off it, Amoros stuck his glove out like a bum accepting a handout. The baseball plopped right in. The brilliant catch was followed by a more brilliant reaction. He immediately wheeled and fired a strike to Reese. Martin had to just stand at second base in frustration, watching Reese relay to Hodges to nab McDougald by a half step.

In the seventh Mantle, batting right-handed, got his pitch, but he had pulled his hamstring and had to shorten his stroke just enough to keep him from powering the ball out, instead popping out to Reese.

The Yankees got their swings and hit some balls well. Podres was throwing hard, challenging them, but he mowed them down until Elston Howard grounded to Reese, and the great Dodger who had seen it all threw him out to give Brooklyn their first world title.

Team Leader

Duke Snider was cursed at an early age, "robbed of the gift of perspective," according to Michael Shapiro in *The Last Good Season.* Growing up in the Los Angeles area, he was "that most envied and exalted of young men: the best ballplayer around."

Snider's dad worked at the Goodyear Tire Company plant. He called his son "Duke," which fit with his athletic manner. Young Snider starred in baseball, basketball, and football, earning 16 letters at Compton High School. He was popular, and met his future wife when they were both high school juniors.

Baseball came easy for him.

"It was fun," he said. "I didn't know what adversity was in baseball when I was a youngster. I always got a hit."

At the age of 17 Snider signed with Brooklyn and went off to play at Newport News, Virginia. After a short navy stint, Snider found himself in a very competitive situation. The Dodgers were loaded. Nobody had more minor league players. Slowly but surely Snider's star rose above the rest until, after a couple of up-and-down seasons, he stuck in Brooklyn in 1949.

Snider initially had trouble handling big-league pitching. Unlike players who struggle on the way up, Snider's great success since his youngest days had not prepared him for failure, which of course is the hobgoblin of big-league life. The good ones succeed roughly three or four out of every 10 tries.

But Branch Rickey knew that Snider was the real deal and built his club around the center fielder. Snider was also an excellent teammate for Robinson. On a team with its share of Southerners, Midwesterners, and East Coasters, it was good for Robinson to have

A smiling Duke Snider clears out his locker after his four homers propelled Brooklyn to the 1955 World Series win over the Yankees.

DID YOU KNOW ... That when Duke Snider was at the top of his game, making $50,000 per year, he complained to Roger Kahn that he was tired of playing baseball? *Collier's* sent Kahn to Los Angeles for an off-season interview, and the subsequent article hit the sports world like a bomb. Snider played an additional nine years in the big leagues.

a fellow Los Angeleno. Snider had seen Robinson play college football. The two helped each other. It was Robinson who taught Snider the patience he needed to hone his competitive juices, to understand that when failure occurs, it must be overcome in order to compete the next day, instead of overwhelming the player.

While Snider would eventually be considered the "team leader," that would happen over time and in accordance with his status as the best hitter and defensive genius in center field.

There were many veterans who Snider learned from early on. He was neither the team leader nor the best player at the beginning. Robinson and shortstop Pee Wee Reese were leaders on a team of strong personalities. Roy Campanella, winning three MVP awards and handling the chores in stalwart manner behind the dish, was their best player.

But as the 1950s played out, it was Snider who emerged. The comparisons became impossible to avoid. Who was the best center fielder: Mickey Mantle of the Yankees, Willie Mays of the Giants, or Snider?

Looking back from the vantage point of history, Mays and Mantle rate ahead of Snider, who was still a Hall of Famer. But Duke was a star before either of those two were established. By the middle of the decade, it was not yet decided who amongst the three really was the best.

Carl Erskine tells a humorous Duke Snider story in *Tales from the Dodger Dugout.* Pee Wee Reese, Rube Walker, Erskine, and Snider would ride together from Brooklyn to the Polo Grounds when they played the Giants. One day Reese was pulled over by a traffic cop on the West Side Highway.

After showing his driver's license, the cop inquired where he worked. Reese said he was with the Dodgers. He introduced his

Greatest Teams of All Time

1. 1927 New York Yankees
2. 1998 New York Yankees
3. 1961 New York Yankees
4. 1975 Cincinnati Reds
5. 1930 Philadelphia A's
6. 1970 Baltimore Orioles
7. 1928 New York Yankees
8. 1955 Brooklyn Dodgers
9. 1942 St. Louis Cardinals
10. 1986 New York Mets

teammates to the cop, who shook hands all around and did not write a ticket.

The next day Snider was handling the driving when he was caught in the same speed trap, but by a different cop. Without being asked, Snider informed the policeman who he and his passengers were. The officer was obviously no Dodger fan.

"I don't like baseball," he said.

"I don't like cops," said Snider. "Gimme that ticket!"

They rode the rest of the way in silence.

Snider's breakout season was 1950, the year Brooklyn lost on the last day to Dick Sisler and Philadelphia. He had hit 23 home runs in 1949, but in '50 slammed 31 with 199 hits, a .321 average, and 107 RBIs.

In 1951 he again drove in more than 100 runs but, like his teammates, faded toward the end when the Giants came out of nowhere to capture the flag. But from 1952 to 1955 he batted over .300 each season. He hit more than 40 home runs every year from 1953 to 1957 and drove in over 100 from 1953 to 1956.

Snider, along with Don Drysdale, was returning home when the Dodgers moved to Los Angeles, but his attitude was different from Dandy Don's. Drysdale was in his early twenties. Snider, even though he had married a California girl, was established with deep roots in the borough, as had most of the veteran Dodgers.

He had been outstanding in the team's final season at Ebbets Field, slamming 40 homers with 92 runs batted in. While Alston saw aging veterans and wanted to engage in a "youth movement," Snider was not part of that movement. He was expected to be a star in L.A., and a box office attraction, as well.

A classic photo in Glenn Stout's *The Dodgers: 120 Years of Dodgers Baseball* shows Snider in a tailored suit with tie clasp standing with two young lovelies wearing Dodger caps and tight shorts. Snider's hair is slicked back and he looks to be "the Duke" in all his glory, his arm around the brunette's waist, the blonde smiling to his left. They are picking chocolates out of a giant box, so that the empty slots spell out "Los Angeles Is Sweet on the Dodgers."

Snider certainly was expected to be the big hometown hero, but the dimensions of the Coliseum rudely awakened him. Many of his home runs had been hit at the bandbox Ebbets Field, which might as well have been built for him. He did not have Wally Moon's "inside-out" swing. He pulled balls to right field that would have been home runs in Brooklyn, but were loud outs at the Coliseum. In order to compensate for the short porch in left, the dimensions to center, right-center, and straightaway right field were cavernous (the right-field line was short but then expanded).

He hit a mere 15 home runs in 1958, although his speed in center was still of great benefit, and his average was a respectable .312. In the world championship season of 1959, Snider hit 23 home runs and batted .308, but by 1962 Willie Davis was a Dodger and Snider was part of the past, not the future.

In his book, *Few and Chosen: Defining Dodgers Greatness across the Eras,* Snider expressed that he liked Charlie Dressen more than Walter Alston. Perhaps the fact that Alston's "youth movement" eventually moved him out of the starting lineup, and then eventually out of Los Angeles, was part of his reasoning.

Ironically, Snider found himself back in New York in 1963, with the fledgling Mets, and then wearing the uniform of the hated Giants in 1964 before hanging 'em up. He finished with 407 career home runs and a .295 average.

Exodus

It all happened so fast. In 1955 there was unmitigated joy when the Dodgers won the World Series. In 1956 the pennant was successfully defended, but a series of bizarre events foreshadowed the great migration west. Sal Maglie became a Dodger. Jackie Robinson was traded to the Giants.

Maglie, considered washed up, arrived when the team was struggling early in 1956. He replaced Billy Loes, the "anti-Maglie." Loes had the talent Maglie did not, but lacked the toughness. He said he never wanted to win 20 games because "then you'll expect me to do it every year."

Maglie inspired the Dodgers, who respected their once-hated rival. He won 13 games. Newcombe had his best season ever, finishing with 27 victories, earning him the first-ever Cy Young as well as Most Valuable Player awards. Brooklyn won a close pennant race, but the season had its share of ups and downs. Among the downs were seven games O'Malley scheduled for them in Jersey City, New Jersey, ostensibly to put the powers that be on notice that he was looking for a new park at Flatbush and Atlantic, or someplace else.

The Series was a polar opposite of 1955: the home-field advantage, the 2–0 advantage, the seven-game winner. Brooklyn won the first two at Ebbets, knocking out Whitey Ford and triumphing despite a gargantuan Mantle homer, which supposedly rattled off of car hoods for "half a minute."

In Game 2 they trailed 6–0 but then knocked Don Larsen from here to Sunday, winning 13–8. But the "great" Don Newcombe was a "fold artist" who did not want to pitch in the Series. He didn't make

That while Walter O'Malley gets almost all the blame for the Dodgers leaving Brooklyn, New York City building czar Robert Moses deserves just as much? Moses held more power in the Big Apple than any politician, granting "yea" or "nay" to all big architectural plans. He completely nixed all of O'Malley's proposed stadium plans. After the Dodgers left, he did approve the building of Shea Stadium in conjunction with the 1964 World's Fair.

it through the second inning of Game 2, but the Dodgers rallied to win. Without him the team was not going to get it done. Ford, his opposite in style, personality, and guts—with ice water running through his veins—beat Brooklyn 5–3. Brooklyn lost Game 4. Alston knew that Newcombe—a 27-game winner, a Cy Young winner, and an MVP winner—lacked heart.

Maglie, a real winner, pitched brilliantly in place of Newcombe in Game 5, but ran into Larsen. Knocked out in Game 2, now he was *perfect*—as in a perfect game. Yanks 2, Dodgers 0.

Game 6 at Ebbets Field was a doozy, with Brooklyn eking out a 1–0 thriller in ten, but they fell flat in a 9–0 Game 7 disaster with Newcombe being knocked out in the fifth inning. Newcombe would have his trophies but no respect. His long bout with alcohol may well trace to his inability to win a single career World Series game, just one or two of which may have given his team...one or two more world championships in addition to the 1955 title.

The famed exhibition to Japan followed the season. Nobody wanted to go. Robinson refused, and despite all his history was unceremoniously dumped a few months later.

The plane stopped in L.A. O'Malley met with L.A. City Councilman Kenneth Hahn, who had been at the World Series, ostensibly trying to talk Washington Senators owner Calvin Griffith into moving to Los Angeles. Giants owner Horace Stoneham was rumored to be interested in California too. O'Malley knew that the prime city in the Golden State was L.A. He wanted it before Griffith or Stoneham claimed it.

Hahn put on a full-court press at that meeting and subsequent others. O'Malley secretly committed to L.A. prior to the 1957 season. O'Malley sweetened the deal by declaring he did not want the city to build him a ballpark. He had had it with the bureaucracy of such a thing. He wanted the land and he would do the rest himself.

Any chance that the Dodgers would stay evaporated when O'Malley sold Ebbets Field to a commercial developer instead of to a competing interest who promised to keep the team in Brooklyn or build on land near La Guardia Airport in Queens.

Throughout 1957 O'Malley pretended to negotiate with the city to stay, but the die was cast. He flew to L.A. again and found the most perfect site for a baseball stadium. Chavez Ravine, sitting adjacent to and on a hilltop overlooking downtown Los Angeles, was criss-crossed by freeways that made it accessible to and from every part of the city and suburb alike. O'Malley then bought the Cubs' longtime L.A. franchise in the Pacific Coast League. The Cubs had held the

Dodgers officials (plus player Junior Gilliam, bottom second from left) depart LaGuardia Airport for Los Angeles on October 23, 1957. Club president Walter O'Malley is at the top right.

Southern California market for years, ever since Phillip Wrigley bought a significant portion of Catalina Island, using it for the team's spring training. (Cubs announcer Ronald Reagan got his start in Hollywood because of it; he went for a lark screen test during the Catalina spring and was signed on.)

O'Malley now owned L.A.'s Wrigley Field, located on Avalon. The Hollywood Stars also played in a stadium where the current CBS TV Center is. But O'Malley had little interest in playing big-league games at the 22,000-seat "little Wrigley." He inquired of the Los Angeles Memorial Coliseum and was told "it holds 100,000 people, but it's a football stadium."

TRIVIA

What did Willie Mays say to Duke Snider the first time Mays saw the short left-field fence at the Coliseum and the wide-open spaces from center (410 feet) to straightaway right field (402 feet compared to 296 at Ebbets)?

Answers to the trivia questions are on pages 178–179

Not any more, thought O'Malley, calculating the monetary difference between 90,000 and 22,000 tickets sold.

In 1973 Martin Scorsese made a Mob movie based on his youth in Little Italy. In the final scene of *Mean Streets,* Robert DeNiro and Harvey Keitel make a suicidal drive, settling an old score with a bad end that can be metaphorically seen from a mile away. Symbolically, the camera captures the passing sign "Last Exit to Brooklyn," which was also the name of a bitter novel written in the 1950s.

O'Malley made his last exit from Brooklyn after the 1957 season. For Brooklyn Dodger fans, the events play out like the Zapruder film, as if in the retelling of the story, somehow it will turn out differently. One myth is that the poor showing of the Dodgers and Giants on the field, which led to lousy attendance (while the Yankees, like the Romans prevailing in a war of attrition over Hannibal, won the pennant and the city), thus effected the move.

O'Malley was committed and had been since before the season. Stoneham was on board with San Francisco his destination. The league approved the move on May 29, 1957. The Giants and Dodgers of the glory days were no more. Both teams looked old. Leo Durocher had been fired. The Giants would venture west with

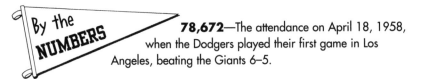

78,672—The attendance on April 18, 1958, when the Dodgers played their first game in Los Angeles, beating the Giants 6–5.

Willie Mays, of course, but it would be a new-look team. So, too, with the Dodgers.

Robinson was gone. There were veterans who would go to L.A. and some would contribute, but none would come close to their Brooklyn days. Their "new look" consisted of young Koufax, whose handsome visage, despite his Brooklyn upbringing, was L.A. all the way. The same with Don Drysdale, a California-bred pitcher. His Van Nuys High School teammate had been a right fielder who then dropped out of the University of Colorado, where he had a baseball scholarship, to pursue acting. His name was Bobby Redford. Another classmate was already an accomplished actress named Natalie Wood.

California was like a magnet, drawing not just the Dodgers but an entire postwar, suburbanized, car-crazy nation to the growing Sunbelt. Gladys Gooding played "Auld Lang Syne" after the last game. The writers, particularly Dick Young of the *New York Daily News,* wrote vicious, horrid articles about O'Malley, the perfect villain. He couldn't care less. He had harnessed the future.

Changes

Change, as they say, is good. Change seemed to be a good thing in the winter of 1957–58 for Roy Campanella, the club's star catcher since 1949. He had to be flexible. Campy had endured the hardships of the old Negro Leagues, then faced further, more difficult challenges following in Jackie Robinson's footsteps.

Walter O'Malley moved the Bums from a stadium where Campanella had hit a majority of his 242 home runs, but now, what was this? The Dodgers would be playing in a football stadium, the Coliseum—and word was that the left-field fence was little-league distance.

Campanella had learned to adapt because he had to, and after winning three National League MVP awards between 1951 and 1955, he was ready for a new challenge. The new challenge was not just about the impending move to L.A. At age 37, Campanella had become a small businessman. He had bought a liquor store in suburban New York, and on an ice-cold January night in 1958, after working the night shift, Roy got in his car for the drive home. He never made it.

His car skidded off the road, rammed into a tree, and the great athlete, a man with cat-like reflexes and the most powerful throwing arm on the senior circuit, was paralyzed.

Change can be tough to swallow. Campanella went through the grueling process of rehab, but along the way discovered something special. Sometime between January 1958 and May 1959, Roy Campanella went from being a suicidal paraplegic, whose wife left him because she could not handle his bouts with depression, to learning that it's good to be alive. In the process, his nurse fell in love

Hall of Fame catcher Roy Campanella won three MVP awards.

with him. They call that the "Florence Nightingale effect," and in Roy's case change again was very good. They were eventually married.

Baseball is rooted in the Eastern mythology of New York City. Cooperstown is a few hours away, and in the 1950s the Yankees, Giants, and Dodgers were building their own wings at the Hall of Fame, with three marquee center fielders named Willie Mays, Mickey Mantle, and Duke Snider. Los Angeles was, well...Hollywood. A nice place to visit, you might even want to live there, but not to be taken seriously, as in major league seriously.

TRIVIA

What was Walter O'Malley's initial plan for television coverage of L.A. Dodger games?

Answers to the trivia questions are on pages 178–179

Perhaps it was on May 7, 1959, that the world first took Los Angeles major league seriously. When former teammate Pee Wee Reese rolled Campy out to home plate, the lights dimmed, and 93,103 fans of the human spirit lit lighters, giving the Coliseum a heavenly appearance, paying a very moving tribute to a man who had played his entire career 3,000 miles away.

They adopted Roy Campanella as one of their own, and they adopted a club that had finished in seventh place in 1958. The Dodgers would go on to break the 90,000 attendance mark several times during their stay in Exposition Park—the '59 All-Star Game, and in three games versus the "Go-Go" Chicago White Sox in that year's fall classic. Whether the players were inspired by Campy and their adopted hometown to win the world championship is grist for speculation, and the stuff of legend.

Duke Snider speculated on what might have been.

"If it hadn't been for the accident," Snider once said, "I think Roy would have played another year or two and then been the first black manager."

Campanella's life was much more than wins, losses, and MVP awards. Another former Dodger, pitcher Joe Black, remembers Hall of Famer Campy this way: "To me, he was the ultimate role model."

Roy's life was memorialized first in his uplifting autobiography, *It's Good to Be Alive*, and later in a television movie of the same name.

Change also came in the form of the West Coast move, which Campy eventually made after all.

He became a fixture at Dodger Stadium, working for the club in an advisory capacity until he passed away from natural causes in 1993. It would seem that Campanella's starry May night in 1959 inspired his team to great heights. The Dodgers were a team in transition. Many of the Brooklyn stars were aging or gone. Some of the young Brooklyn hopefuls emerged as stars. A new group also began to assert themselves.

The town took to the team in the biggest way possible. Hollywood stars Danny Kaye, Jimmy Stewart, Burt Lancaster, Jack Lemmon, Gene Autry, Groucho Marx, and Ray Bolger were fixtures at Dodger games.

Outfielder Wally Moon hit 19 homers and batted .302 to lead the team. He had the perfect inside-out left-handed swing, resulting in high, arching fly balls that cleared the short in distance, but tall in height left-field fence at the Coliseum.

Moon, pitcher Larry Sherry, new shortstop Maury Wills, pitchers Don Drysdale and Sandy Koufax, and Campy's replacement behind the plate, John Roseboro, kept the team in contention until San Francisco slumped in September.

After tying Milwaukee through 154 games, L.A. beat the Braves twice to capture the league crown. With enormous crowds spurring L.A. on at the Coliseum, they managed to beat the "Go-Go" White Sox in six games to capture the world championship. What Brooklyn fans had waited some 51 years for, Los Angeles was given in just their second season.

The star of the Series, and in fact the glue of the pitching staff down the stretch, was relief pitcher Larry Sherry. Sherry hailed from Fairfax High in L.A. More great athletes came from the American West in the 20th century, mostly from California, than any place in the world. A new dynamic played itself out in L.A., that of the homegrown hero. New York did not produce a large number of great baseball players. There were some, to be sure, but nothing like L.A.

More than 2 million fans attended Dodger games in 1959. It was the great incentive, all the way around, that spurred the creation of Dodger Stadium. Bad press regarding the relocation of Mexican immigrants living in Chavez Ravine had been a setback, until readers of the *Los Angeles Times* had the record set a little straighter. Few owned their property, most lived in makeshift homes, one tenant owned 11 slum buildings throughout the city, and few were U.S. citizens.

A Baseball Palace

The Los Angeles Memorial Coliseum may or may not be the most famous football stadium. It gets competition from Lambeau Field in Green Bay, Notre Dame Stadium in South Bend, and a few others. It is the most famous *sports* stadium because so many different things have happened there.

Yankee Stadium is the most famous baseball stadium, because of the great success of the club and the legendary players who have worn their pinstripes. But the *best* baseball facility ever built is Dodger Stadium.

There are challengers to that title. Oriole Field at Camden Yards and AT&T Park in San Francisco are recent stadiums that combine all the best elements of old and new. AT&T's waterfront location is an added, spectacular benefit.

But Dodger Stadium is special. Opened in 1962, it is now "old" enough to be a place hanging with history, which of course is a testament to the great teams and games played there over the years. But its uniqueness is in its design, its architecture, and in its location. It is a place of wonder.

First and foremost, it sits on a rise about two miles from downtown L.A. While it is totally surrounded by urbanity—freeways, a teeming population, skyscrapers, sprawl—one travels up a slight but steady palm tree–lined grade in order to get there. The immediate surroundings create the illusion, in true movie style, of a park in...*a park*, amid foothills and foliage. At the same time, fans leaving the stadium at night are met by a spectacular view of the well-lit downtown high rises, which has gotten more spectacular over the decades.

The awe-inspiring nature of the stadium—and this is still from the outside—is made apparent adjacent to the Dodger offices, where many advance tickets are sold and fans traverse a steep stairwell under clusters of greenery designed to resemble the Biblical Hanging Gardens of Babylon. It is not an exaggeration to say that the place gives people the impression that they are on a fabulous John Huston or Cecil B. DeMille movie set.

Like a "shining city on a hill," spectacular Dodger Stadium indeed does sit atop a plateau overlooking the downtown L.A. skyscrapers.

Dodger Stadium's first impression is its cleanliness. Candlestick Park, built in San Francisco two years earlier, immediately looked old and garbage-strewn. Dodger Stadium appears to be a place in which one could eat dinner off its polished floors.

It is and continues to be a stadium built entirely for the benefit of fan comfort and viewing pleasure. Many ballparks in Cincinnati, Texas, Pittsburgh, Seattle, Philadelphia, and elsewhere have been built and torn down since because they failed to accommodate baseball fans. Dodger Stadium is a baseball-only facility that does not foist a 50-yard-line seat on fans who want to see a good angle of the pitcher.

Its parking lot is spacious, with easy access to all the major freeways. Despite long distances and heavy traffic, the stadium is as accessible as any place can be in a place as huge as greater Los Angeles. Season-ticket holders' parking lots are color-corresponded to their seats, allowing for easy access in and out.

Seventy percent of the seats are "on" the infield, all with unobstructed views and comfortable, wide seats—a most welcome early feature for fans used to sitting on hard, wooden benches, often behind pillars blocking the field of play. Dodger Stadium was the first park to offer luxury boxes, as well as the field-level seats made so famous by television. That was a feature Walter O'Malley liked from his team's tour of Japan.

The stadium club is posh, and the Diamond Room caters to stars and celebrities who need a private place to hobnob with each other. Still, a thrill for average fans has always been the numerous "star sightings" at a stadium located just 15 minutes from Hollywood Boulevard. Despite the exclusive nature of celebrity in L.A., the comingling of average fans with the rich and famous has always been an easygoing affair, with few occasions of trouble. A sense of democracy pervades Dodger Stadium, where fans of wide diversity share their love of baseball. It could be argued with great validity that relations between

TRIVIA

After the Dodgers' disappointing seventh-place finish in 1958, whose name was most regularly mentioned as the likely replacement for Walt Alston?

Answers to the trivia questions are on pages 178–179

By the
NUMBERS

100 million—The number of people who had attended games at Dodger Stadium entering the 2001 season (2.68 million per year for 39 years).

whites and Latinos in Southern California, which have improved greatly over the years, owe as much of this to the shared Dodger Stadium experience as any other calculation.

Warm L.A. weather has always increased the sense of paradise, especially at night, which is normally shirt-sleeve comfortable. Day games are fairly rare (the team was the first to play Saturday night games, and plays few weekday games), but feature a relaxed, beach-attire quality to them. Naturally, people-watching is an art form at Dodger Stadium.

But perhaps Dodger Stadium's greatest attribute is its ability to convey wholesomeness. In this respect, the Dodgers have always been unique, and the contributions of Vin Scully certainly are to be credited. But the stadium itself does something very special. It is not unlike the speech that James Earl Jones makes at the end of *Field of Dreams,* in which he states that fans will come to the ballpark built by Kevin Costner's character to find something "good," to discover part of their lost youth; that the experience will be like "dipping themselves in magic waters."

Few if any sports stadiums convey this kind of nostalgic joy, but Dodger Stadium has it in droves.

Dodger Stadium is an oasis in Los Angeles. Fans live in the real L.A. world of traffic, smog, gangs, corruption, greed, and racial animosity. Amidst all of this, a man can take his family to Dodger Stadium and recapture, for a few lost hours, the "magic waters" of innocence. Walter O'Malley, a man of greed and corruption, managed, despite himself, to build a baseball temple of joy to embrace the very best elements of a game, a city, and its people.

Summer of '62

The year 1962 is the dividing line in Dodger baseball history. After four years at the Coliseum, which despite much carping served its purpose well, the team moved into Dodger Stadium. But 1962 is one of those years that stands out in the mind's eye as unique, like 1927 when Babe Ruth hit 60 and Charles Lindbergh crossed the Atlantic or 1945 when the war was won.

So 1962 is now remembered as the last year of innocence, before JFK's assassination and the Vietnam War (although the Cuban Missile Crisis was a heavy dose of reality). Old footage from '62, however, demonstrates a "surfer" innocence that does not exist a few years later, when the antiwar protest movement took to the streets like a pack of wolves.

Like 1951, for the Dodgers it was a season of intense baseball rivalry that ended in bitter defeat at the hands of the Giants. The new location, the new stadium, and the new fan sensibilities were extensions of John McGraw, Bill Terry, and Leo Durocher, who was in actuality part of it again, this time as a "celebrity coach" seemingly placed on Walter Alston's staff for the express purpose of threatening Alston's job.

Despite defeat, the 1962 Dodgers were one of the best teams in the franchise's history, East or West. In many ways they were better than the world champion teams that followed in succeeding years. They were loaded with talent.

Don Drysdale won 25 games, his only Cy Young award, and may have had his best year. Shortstop Maury Wills broke Ty Cobb's single-season stolen-base record with 104 en route to the MVP award. Outfielder Tommy Davis had one of the best offensive

DID YOU KNOW ... That the Dodgers had a musical act that played in Las Vegas? Shortstop Maury Wills played the banjo during Dinah Shore's act at the Riviera, while Sandy Koufax, Don Drysdale, and Willie Davis crooned before the Baseball Writers' Banquet, which also featured Danny Thomas and Bob Newhart.

seasons in Dodger history, leading the league in batting (.346) and hits (230), with 27 homers and 153 RBIs. Other major contributors were catcher John Roseboro, infielder Junior Gilliam, and outfielders Willie Davis (.285, great defense) and Frank Howard (31 homers, 119 RBIs).

The Dodgers of the 1960s are considered "Hitless Wonders" who scratched out 1–0 victories on the strength of Drysdale's and Koufax's pitching, which is fairly true as it relates to the 1965–66 teams. But the '62 club (102–63) was an offensive powerhouse; a complete team of power, speed, defense, and pitching.

On the mound, relievers Ron Perranoski (20 saves) and Larry Sherry (7–3, 3.20 ERA) were effective, as were Johnny Podres, Stan Williams, and Ed Roebuck. So how did they manage to lose a heart-breaking pennant chase to San Francisco? First, it was the best team in San Francisco history. Second, Sandy Koufax, or the *lack* of Sandy Koufax.

Koufax, the perennial prospect who Alston thought lacked competitive fire, was as spectacular in the first half of the season as any of his three Cy Young years that followed. He struck out 18 Chicago Cubs players in nine innings, tying the all-time record. He threw a no-hitter against the Mets. (When the Dodgers and Giants returned to New York to play the brand new expansion team, they were met by huge crowds who cheered and booed their old heroes.)

By midseason, Koufax led the league in earned-run average, had won 14 games, and was threatening to become the game's first 30-game winner in almost 30 years, as well as being close to breaking Rube Waddell's 1904 record of 349 strikeouts (a disputed figure; Bob Feller struck out 348 in 1946). But "Dandy Sandy's" finger had a blood clot that doctors said was close to gangrene and, if not medicated, might have to be amputated. He was effectively done for the season, and the San Francisco Giants, just as their New York counterparts had done in 1951, slowly crept back into the race. The 20-year-old Willie Mays was now a veteran superstar, the best player in the game.

The Giants actually had gotten off to a good start and were in contention when Koufax's injury ended his year (he pitched in some late-season games but was ineffective). It was a Dodger surge *after* the injury that set San Francisco back. With 13 games left, L.A. led by four. Still, had Koufax been around to win an additional 10 to 15 games in July, August, and September, there never would have been a race.

Enormous crowds came out to Dodger Stadium every night. All previous season attendance records fell in 1962. Until the late 1980s, only the Dodgers would break those records. They thrilled to "Big D," Drysdale, and Wills's pursuit of Cobb's mark. They were the darlings of the jet set—actors, models, and singers who glamorized Dodger Stadium.

The party was interrupted when San Francisco caught fire at the end. Alston threw Koufax a few times but he was unable to get anybody out. With three games left, the Dodgers led by two and

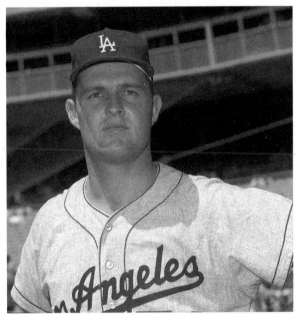

Hall of Fame twirler Don Drysdale symbolized the Dodgers in California.

198,000—The number of fans who saw the first five games ever played by the Dodgers and Giants versus the expansion New York Mets at the Polo Grounds in May 1962.

everybody just wanted them to hold on. Drysdale, overworked in Koufax's absence, was stuck at 25 wins and unable to get that key 26th. Perranoski was also overpitched to the point of ineffectiveness. The presence of Durocher was a distraction, with a large portion of the media ready to call for Alston's ouster and Durocher's hiring.

Alston was totally out of character in L.A.: a quiet, unassuming Midwesterner. Durocher, who palled around with Frank Sinatra, was seemingly born for the Hollywood limelight.

In a final day eerily reminiscent of the spectacular last regular season games of 1951, the Dodgers lost a heartbreaker to St. Louis, 1–0, while Mays ended a thriller with Houston by homering to propel the Giants to a 2–1 win. Another playoff.

"Wanted," wrote Jim Murray in the *Los Angeles Times,* "one nearly new 1962 National League pennant, slightly soiled with tear stain in center. Last seen blowing toward San Francisco... Warning: if you return pennant to Dodgers direct, be sure to tape it to their hands."

In the first playoff game, Koufax was drubbed and Billy Pierce shut out L.A. to give San Francisco an 8–0 win at Dodger Stadium. History records show that Koufax is a baseball deity in L.A., considered one of the great big-game pitchers the game has ever known. This is a well-deserved reputation, but in late 1962 Alston was not the only one who doubted the severity of his injury in an era of "suck it up and play hurt" managers. It has been suggested that anti-Semitism played a role in Alston's—and others'—thinking.

The truth is, it was Don Drysdale, healthy but exhausted mentally and physically, who failed the team when most needed down the stretch. He was hit hard in Game 2, but the Giants, as if they did not want to win the pennant, allowed a 5–0 lead to slip through their fingers in an 8–7 loss.

When Los Angeles took a 4–2 lead into the ninth of the last playoff game, the similarities to 1951 were just too horrible to contemplate. If

TRIVIA

Where did Sandy Koufax live when he played in Los Angeles?

Answers to the trivia questions are on pages 178–179

Los Angelenos thought they were immune from the kind of heartbreak seemingly reserved for the denizens of Brooklyn, they were rudely mistaken. There was no dramatic "shot heard 'round the world," just a tired Dodger bullpen that could not throw strikes, bad defense, questionable managing, and a few timely hits, namely by Mays. Giants 6, Dodgers 4.

What followed was one of baseball's worst postgame meltdowns. With the clubhouse doors locked, players started drinking, shouting, and cursing, mostly at Alston, who locked himself in his office. Chief among the complaints was his refusal to go to Drysdale, who claimed he had an inning left in him, in the ninth. Drysdale tried to break Alston's door down, which is curious because they would not have been in this position had he pitched worth a darn down the stretch, and it was his wholesale inability to get anybody out that probably colored the decision not to use him.

Accusations ran rampant, all around the theme that the $12,000 that goes with a pennant (significant money in the '62 pay scale) had been blown by Walt. Like Javert from *Les Miserables,* Durocher played the baseball version of *j'accuse,* his goal being Alston's head under the guillotine, symbolically. Alston looked to be gone, but general manager Buzzie Bavasi maintained his cool amidst "the terrors," keeping him on to the great good of the club's future.

New York, New York

The Dodgers won the 1959 World Series at the L.A. Coliseum, which is a significant and interesting part of their history, but 1963 was the year they reached the Promised Land. In 1959 the Yankees had a rare down year, allowing the White Sox to capture the flag (thus denying a first L.A.–N.Y. fall classic). In 1962 the Dodgers missed a chance to play New York in the Series when they folded down the stretch, setting up a classic S.F.–N.Y. seven-game tussle, won by the Yankees.

But in 1963 everything came together in a manner more perfect than any fiction writer could conjure. It was a year in which the Los Angeles Dodgers returned to the "scene of the crime"—in more ways than one—New York City. With their Brooklyn-born ace, Koufax, and his former Brooklyn teammate, Drysdale, they beat the vaunted Yankees on their home turf. In so doing, they removed any doubts from 1962, not to mention exorcising all remaining ghosts in a still-haunted Dodger attic. In Hollywood terms, they were like the hot young star of a big blockbuster whose acting chops are still considered suspect, but after following that up with an Academy Award a few years later, he has *arrived!*

The Dodgers had arrived.

Much of the credit goes to Bavasi, who made the correct choice in keeping Alston and jettisoning Durocher's cabal: Stan Williams, Larry Burright, and Duke Snider were assayed, whether validly or not, with much of the 1962 blame on the field, or for clubhouse dissension off it.

Alston was urged to find greater understanding of Koufax, the "new breed" of ballplayer who did not jump up and down, swear, and spit tobacco juice. Sandy's intellectualism and Jewish background

All–1960s
Dodgers Team

Position	Name
Pitcher	Don Drysdale
Pitcher	Sandy Koufax
Pitcher	Claude Osteen
Relief Pitcher	Ron Perranoski
Catcher	John Roseboro
First Baseman	Wes Parker
Second Baseman	Jim Lefebvre
Third Baseman	Junior Gilliam
Shortstop	Maury Wills
Outfielder	Tommy Davis
Outfielder	Willie Davis
Outfielder	Frank Howard
Utility Player	Ron Fairly
Manager	Walt Alston

was originally seen by Alston as the sign of a lack of heart, but Alston was well rounded enough to adjust his thinking. Drysdale was of course far too valuable to unload despite his October clubhouse outburst, but his anger was attributable to what Alston saw as a savage, yet admirable, desire for victory.

Everything hinged on Koufax, and when he came out strong and healthy in the spring, throwing an early no-hit game versus San Francisco, things were looking up. St. Louis hit the ground running, sweeping L.A., but in May the Dodgers turned it around. Alston, tired of the griping and complaining, broke his usual silence, challenging the entire team to take a shot at him if they were men enough. None did. After the endless rumors of Durocher's "unfriendly takeover" boiled in July, the team surged. St. Louis fell in three straight. A friendly schedule featured the Houston Colt .45s and the Mets, contributing to an L.A. winning streak. Koufax hurled three straight shutouts. After winning 17 of 20, Los Angeles pulled to a seven-and-a-half-game lead over San Francisco.

In September, however, it was "déjà vu all over again," as Yogi Berra once said. With a six-game edge over now second-place St. Louis, Los Angeles withstood a 19-of-20 surge from Stan Musial's Cardinals, but they held on to grab 13 of 19 themselves. Leading by one entering St. Louis, Alston's job was on the line. His constant platooning was blamed for the reduced offensive production, but Johnny Podres and Koufax stifled Redbird bats. In the finale, L.A. won on Cardinal mistakes in extra innings. The Dodgers cruised after that to 99 wins and the World Series, which opened at Yankee Stadium.

The opener featured 20-game winners Koufax versus Whitey Ford. It was an instant classic. Ford was a Hall of Fame lock by this time, and just as much of a lock to win at the Stadium. A matchup of the old vet with the young superstar, coming in with 25 wins, 11 shutouts, another no-hitter, 306 strikeouts, and a 1.88 ERA (all of which would later earn him the Cy Young and MVP awards) was as good as it gets.

Ford sat L.A. down in the first with the dispatch of a commuter picking up the train to Greenwich. Then Koufax mowed down New York's best in the first inning: three strikeouts on 10 pitches. Yankee Stadium was silenced. L.A. pieced together a rally against the stunned Ford to lead 4–0, and Koufax thoroughly dominated. He had nine strikeouts through four innings, a no-hitter into the fifth, and finished with a World Series–record 15 Ks, which, as Vin Scully liked to point out, went with the first letter of his last name.

Statistically, Koufax had better games—in the 1965 World Series, or his perfect game—but all things considered, beating the Mickey Mantle-Roger Maris Yankees, with Ford on the mound at Yankee Stadium, when it counted most, was his greatest moment.

Podres and the speed of Wills propelled the 4–1 win in Game 2 at Yankee Stadium, the scene of Johnny's classic 1955 Series-clincher. Don Drysdale outdueled 21-game-winner Jim Bouton at Dodger Stadium. With

TRIVIA

What did the famed quotemeister Yogi Berra have to say after facing Sandy Koufax in the 1963 World Series?

Answers to the trivia questions are on pages 178–179

Koufax on tap next, Yankee manager Ralph Houk remarked, "Well, we've got 27 more outs."

L.A. broke up a 1–1 tie on some mishaps in the seventh, and that was all Koufax needed. He mowed New York down as if they were a high school team, not the fabled Bronx Bombers, two-time defending world champions, a team of fear and conquest.

The four-game sweep seemed utterly unbelievable. Here was the first-ever New York–Los Angeles World Series, and like the

Sandy Koufax embraces catcher John Roseboro after beating the Yankees to sweep the 1963 World Series at Dodger Stadium.

Yankee-Giant classic of 1962 and the many donnybrooks the two teams had fought in New York, it seemed destined to go to the wire.

Despite Koufax's total regular season domination, it was not until he dispatched the seemingly unbeatable Yankees without apparently breaking a sweat that his legend was made. Alston, who, despite having won two previous world championships, had less respect than Rodney Dangerfield, said, "This makes up for everything."

This was a shining moment: a World Series win to christen Dodger Stadium; a young team; Koufax and Drysdale just reaching stardom and looking to be able to do it for another decade.

Bavasi made no changes, and why should he? Koufax opened 1964 with a shutout, but shortly thereafter felt something pop in his pitching arm. Cortisone proved to be a short-term cure, allowing Koufax to win 19 games (one being a third no-hitter) against five losses with a 1.74 ERA. Unfortunately, he did all of that before September. The cortisone hid the pain, but all the while Koufax, who needed to rest the injury, was developing arthritis. It finally swelled "like a waterlogged log," ending his—and his team's—season.

St. Louis won a tight pennant race and beat the Yankees—suddenly old and making their "last hurrah"—in the World Series.

"Hitless Wonders"

There have been many great "one-two" pitching combinations throughout baseball history. Christy Mathewson and "Iron Joe" McGinnity of the McGraw's Giants, of course. Chief Bender and Eddie Plank of Connie Mack's A's. Waite Hoyt and Herb Pennock of the Yankees are worthy.

But the Koufax-Drysdale duo stands out for several reasons. They were, seemingly, made for Hollywood. Drysdale was 6'6", with the good looks to match his high school teammate Robert Redford. He looked like the hero of cowboy movies, and indeed wore a six-shooter on screen.

Koufax was also a favorite with the ladies, a bachelor who made brief forays into acting, but was ultimately too shy to be a leading man or a Sunset Strip playboy in the manner of his contemporary, Angel southpaw Bo Belinsky.

Being in L.A. at the height of Dodger glory, with all the media attention that does not exist in Milwaukee or most other big-league cities, these two were the subject of that extra hoopla. But they earned it on the field, particularly as it relates to their extraordinary accomplishments in the face of low run support from 1963–66.

Drysdale compiled a 2.95 career earned-run average, but a symbol of his lack of offensive support comes from the fact that only a 3–3 record matches his 2.95 World Series ERA. A premature injury held him to 209 career wins. He won 17 at Brooklyn in 1957, 17 for the '59 world champs, then 25 with a 2.83 ERA in 1962. His 19–17 (2.63 ERA) and 18–16 (2.18 ERA) records in 1963–64 were marked by a frustrating lack of support when he was on the mound.

In 1965 he simply pitched too well for the low run output to matter (23–12, 2.77 ERA), but in 1966 a slight drop in effectiveness (3.42 ERA) gave him no leeway in a 13–16 season. In 1968 he was as good as it gets, tossing six straight shutouts (a big-league record 58⅔ scoreless innings), but his 2.15 ERA was only good enough to garner him a 14–12 mark.

The image of the "Hitless Wonders" winning pennants on the strength of Koufax's and Drysdale's 1–0 and 2–1 complete-game efforts covers the period from 1963 to 1966. In the '63 World Series, Drysdale won Game 3, 1–0; Koufax, the decider, 2–1. The 1966 World Series loss to Baltimore consisted of two 1–0 games too.

But it was the 1965 season that symbolized the team. Durocher was finally out of Alston's hair. Whether Koufax was better in '65 than he had been in 1963, and whether Drysdale was better that year than he had been in 1962, is immaterial to the fact that they were more dominant in 1965 when they had to be than they were in any other season.

Don Drysdale embraces Sandy Koufax after another big win during the world championship 1965 campaign.

Previous Dodger teams, which were not exactly powerhouses, looked like "Murderer's Row" compared to the 1965 version. It was a pitcher's era, anyway. It would all culminate by 1968—the "Year of the Pitcher"—and after that the mound would be lowered to increase offense.

Dodger Stadium's dimensions were friendlier to pitchers then (the fences were later brought in to accommodate the power of Steve Garvey, Ron Cey, Reggie Smith, and Dusty Baker). The ball did not carry as well in the smoggy night air of the 1960s, and of course the team played almost all their games after dark.

In looking at the statistics, it seems hard to believe that L.A. (97–65) could beat out San Francisco (95–67) in 1965 and again in 1966. In '65 Koufax was 26–8 with a 2.04 earned-run average. Drysdale was 23–12. But the Giants' Juan Marichal was 22–13, with effective support from Bob Shaw, Ron Herbel, Bob Bolin, and Gaylord Perry. L.A.'s leading hitter, Tommy Davis, suffered a season-ending injury early in 1965 (ultimately costing him a possible Hall of Fame career). Ron Fairly was their best hitter with a .274 average, nine homers, and 70 runs batted in. First baseman Wes Parker (.238), second baseman Jim Lefebvre (.250), shortstop Maury Wills (.286, 94 stolen bases), outfielder Willie Davis (.238), left fielder Lou Johnson (.259), and catcher John Roseboro provided the "offense."

In San Francisco, Willie Mays was hitting 52 home runs with 112 RBIs and a .317 average. Willie McCovey contributed 39 homers. Third baseman Jim Ray Hart slammed 23 homers and drove in 96 runs. Catcher Tom Haller's .251 average with 16 homers would have been considered Ruthian by Dodger standards.

In 1966 it was more of the same, but even more astounding. Los Angeles (95–67) again edged out San Francisco (93–68). Koufax was 27–9 with a 1.73 earned-run average, but Drysdale was 13–16. Was Dodger pitching that much better than the

TRIVIA

Sandy Koufax did not pitch Game 1 of the 1965 World Series in observance of Yom Kippur. After Don Drysdale was hit hard in an 8–2 loss, what did he say to Walt Alston?

Answers to the trivia questions are on pages 178–179

2.81—The Dodgers team earned-run average in 1965.

Giants', who featured Marichal (25–6) and Perry (21–8)? L.A. did improve at the plate in 1966. Parker hit .253. Lefebvre struck 24 homers. Wills still was a stolen-base threat. Fairly was a .288 hitter, followed by Davis (.284), Johnson (.272), and Roseboro (.276). Nobody outside of Lefebvre hit 20 home runs. San Francisco featured Mays (37–103–.288), McCovey (36–96–.295), Hart (33–93–.285), Haller (27 homers), plus Jim Davenport. They had two great starting pitchers and power. The mythology of the era is that the Dodger defense was highly superior, but it was really about average, not particularly better than the Giants. Mays was the best who ever lived in center field. McCovey was an excellent first baseman (although not as good as Wes Parker). Davenport, who alternated with Hart, was a fine third sacker. Maury Wills was not a tremendous fielding shortstop. Roseboro was not better than Haller behind the plate.

How did Alston manage to beat Herman Franks's team two years in a row (and three out of four)? Obviously, 90 percent of that answer, especially in 1965, is "Koufax and Drysdale." In '65 Gaylord Perry had not yet fully come into his own, while young Claude Osteen made his Dodger debut at 15–15. Perranoski was a solid closer with 17 saves and a 2.24 ERA.

Offensively, Lou Johnson was a Dodger sparkplug. They bunted, played hit-and-run, and of course stole bases. They were an aggressive team that played "National League baseball," while the Giants tried to be a West Coast version of the Yankees in a park unsuited for the long ball. San Francisco also suffered from the losses of Orlando Cepeda and Felipe Alou in ill-advised trades, possibly because the team's ethnic makeup was too Latino for some old-time people.

One other intangible entered into play: the ugly Marichal-Roseboro bat incident. In August of 1965, before a packed house at Candlestick Park, Marichal perceived that Roseboro's throw back to Koufax nicked his ear. Enraged, he whirled and clobbered the Dodger catcher over the head with his bat. A melee ensued. Koufax, his concentration broken, allowed a game-deciding homer to Mays, but in the long run Marichal's suspension and a determined Dodger club bent on revenge were enough for L.A. to overcome San Francisco's challenge.

In 1966, when Perry flourished, L.A. countered with rookie Don Sutton (12 wins), Osteen (17 wins), and new reliever Phil Regan (14–1, 21 saves, 1.62 ERA). The dropoff after Marichal and Perry was too great for the Giants with their average bullpen. Alston was obviously superior to Franks.

Koufax tossed a perfect game against the Cubs in 1965 while breaking the single-season strikeout record previously held by Rube Waddell (349, a disputed 1904 figure) with 382. In the World Series versus Minnesota, the Dodgers lost the first two while Koufax sat out in honor of Yom Kippur, but then Osteen responded with a shutout, Drysdale beat Mudcat Grant 7–2, and Koufax threw a 7–0 shutout at Dodger Stadium. Pitching on two days' rest in Game 7 at Metropolitan Stadium, Koufax's 2–0 win marks one of his great moments.

In 1966 Koufax and Drysdale held out together to force O'Malley to pay them market value before signing. This act did not affect Koufax, but did seem to set Drysdale back. The Baltimore Orioles were up to the pitching challenge in the 1966 World Series. The Dodger defense let Koufax down and young Jim Palmer beat them, 6–0. Baltimore won Games 3 and 4, 1–0, to sweep the Series.

After the Series, Koufax announced his retirement, stating that his arm pain was unbearable, he hated being high all the time from a constant intake of new pain prescriptions, and he did not want to suffer pain his whole life. He won three Cy Young awards (1963, 1965–66) and one MVP award (1963). He was elected to the Hall of Fame in 1972. Drysdale entered Cooperstown in 1984.

The Real "Dr. K"

"If you had seen Sandy Koufax the first time I saw him, you never would have imagined that he would become what he became—the greatest pitcher I've ever seen and possibly the greatest ever," wrote Duke Snider (with Phil Pepe) in *Few and Chosen: Defining Dodgers Greatness Across the Era.*

Snider's reference to Koufax and his place in baseball history creates an odd argument. On the one hand, Koufax was the greatest. On the other hand, he was not. Baseball historians, when factoring in all the criteria—eras, "dead balls," big parks, small parks, equipment, night games, steroids, and all the rest—point to Koufax's dominance from 1963 to 1966 and state, correctly in this author's view, that for this period of time none have ever been better. That period can actually be extended to 1962, because he was as good in the first half of that season as in the other four, but like 1964—when an injury ended his season early—physical ailments limited him to the first half. It cost his team the pennant and led Walt Alston to question Koufax's toughness.

Judging baseball pitchers is a tricky business. The game is so steeped in tradition and lore that its early heroes are well known, their exploits written in stone. Basketball certainly does not revere its early stars who, aside from Purdue's John Wooden in the 1930s perhaps, are all but unknown. Little credence is given the exploits of hoopsters prior to the mid-1950s or even the 1960s.

Football has more tradition, but the mind's eye has a hard time grappling with the idea that Jim Thorpe, Red Grange, or Bronko Nagurski have the size, speed, and power of Barry Sanders. Yet Babe Ruth is routinely viewed as baseball's greatest player. Koufax's

As this photo details, Sandy Koufax's pitching motion might have been the most perfect in the game's history. He made full use of his strong legs, and he used an overhand motion that came at hitters like an uncoiled spring, releasing a 100-mph fastball.

By the NUMBERS

3—The number of errors made by center fielder Willie Davis in the fifth inning of Game 2 of the 1966 World Series, a 6–0 loss to Baltimore at Dodger Stadium. In Sandy Koufax's final appearance, he was locked in a shutout duel with 20-year-old Jim Palmer until Davis, one of baseball's finest center fielders, lost two balls in "the fierce, smog-glazed sun," according to Roger Angell in *The Summer Game*, followed by "his first really unforgivable play—an angry little-league heave into the Dodger dugout..." Overall, six Dodger errors undid Koufax's usual strong pitching. Dodger fans "cheered bitterly every time Willie Davis caught the ball in the between-inning warmups," but he responded "with grace" to what Angell said was a postgame "reportorial cross-examination that would have done credit to Eichmann's prosecutors." As if to mock himself, Davis later made one of the best catches in World Series history, robbing Boog Powell of a homer in the Game 4 1–0 loss at Memorial Stadium.

statistics are compared to the likes of Christy Mathewson, Walter Johnson, Cy Young, Grover Cleveland Alexander, and later Lefty Grove. Those guys pitched in an era in which 30-game winners were common (there were even a few 40-game winners).

After World War II the game changed in many ways, integration being the biggest, but equipment and playing conditions marking major improvements. Koufax pitched every four days. Today pitchers go every fifth. He had an effective bullpen corps behind him, although he went the distance routinely (unlike even the greatest of current-day hurlers).

Koufax never really got close to winning 30 games, even though Denny McLain proved it to be possible two years after Koufax retired. In comparing his career, the astute historian must judge his short-term record with the body of work of other all-time greats. This requires a balancing act. Almost everybody who played with him or faced him said he was the best they ever saw and probably the best ever, which counts for a lot.

As great as they were, nobody would argue that Warren Spahn and Steve Carlton ever dominated as thoroughly as Koufax, yet it is not inconceivable to state that these two, along with Lefty Grove, might be considered a notch above Koufax in the pantheon of all-time greatness. The question comes down to longevity and how

IF ONLY . . . Sandy Koufax and Don Drysdale had not retired early due to injury, the Dodgers might have been a dynasty well into the 1970s. Koufax was 30 when he retired in 1966. Had he pitched until he was 38, that would have been 1974. Drysdale was 32 upon his 1969 retirement, so he would have been 37 in 1974. Pitching at peak levels in 1967 and 1968 might not have been enough to give L.A. pennants over St. Louis, but it probably would have made them West Division champs in 1969 and 1971. With their improved offense, they might have been contenders in 1972 and maybe champs in '73. Nobody was going to beat Cincinnati in 1970. L.A. won the pennant as it was in '74.

much value is placed upon it. A pitcher's place on the all-time strikeout list and whether he won 300 games or not are thought to be the criteria that differentiates the legends from each other.

In this regard, Tom Seaver and Roger Clemens (300-game winners) are considered greater than Bob Gibson, Jim Palmer, and Juan Marichal, but it is not that cut and dried. Nobody would say that Don Sutton, a member of the 300-win club, was greater than Gibson, Palmer, and Marichal, and maybe not as good as Drysdale (who won 209 games before a career-ending injury). Even Clemens's gaudy record of 341 lifetime wins entering 2006 and his seven Cy Young Awards suffer the unfortunate scrutiny of steroid allegations. Fair or not fair, the longevity of Clemens, Randy Johnson, and other current pitchers raises the steroid question, but of course Spahn pitched well into his forties with no chemical help.

Koufax posted ERAs under 2.00 three times (2.04 in what arguably was his best year, 1965). He set the season strikeout mark at 382 in '65 and passed the 300 mark three of four years (his 1964 injury prevented a possible fourth), but Nolan Ryan broke Koufax's strikeout record in 1973 and set career marks that seem as unreachable as Cy Young's 511 career wins.

Low ERAs were not unusual in Koufax's era. Gibson's 1.12 of 1968 was insane. Luis Tiant, Dean Chance, and others posted ERAs lower than Koufax's lowest (1.73 in 1966). In later years, Greg Maddux and Clemens were as statistically hard to score on.

What was more valuable to his team and more impressive on the whole: Seaver's consistent excellence from the late 1960s to the early

1980s, or Koufax's short run? Seaver won three Cy Young Awards, as did Koufax (but in Koufax's day there was only one for all of baseball, not for each league). Seaver's record begs comparison with Clemens, and again the question of steroids rears its ugly head: what if Seaver had juiced? How much harder would he have thrown? How many more years could he have pitched? How effective would he have been at the end, when his great skills deteriorated after going 14–2 in the strike-shortened 1981 campaign?

Like Super Bowl quarterbacks, of course, greatness is measured in its best way on the greatest of stages, and in this regard Koufax has few equals. In World Series play, he was one of if not the best ever. He was a pure clutch pitcher. His postseason record dwarfs that of Seaver, Clemens, and Carlton.

He is to be listed in that shortest grouping of "big game" hurlers that includes Christy Mathewson (three shutouts in the 1905 World Series), Whitey Ford (who was used by Casey Stengel mostly at home, where he was seemingly unbeatable), Bob Gibson (the hero of the 1964 and '67 Series, maybe even better in noble '68 defeat), and Catfish Hunter (whose A's teams won on the strength of pitching much as Koufax's Dodgers did).

"It's hard to imagine any pitcher in the history of baseball being more dominating than Koufax was in those four years," wrote Snider of his 1963–66 run. Statistically, Johnson, Mathewson, Alexander, Young, and later Grove and Bob Feller had similar stretches. There is analysis that favors Koufax and analysis that favors the others.

In Koufax's favor is the fact that the game was fully integrated with blacks and Latinos by his day. Further augmenting his case is his big-game record and the fact that his team routinely failed to give him run support (although Drysdale had more to complain about than Koufax did). He certainly did not pitch in the dead-ball era. But he enjoyed the advantage of pitching mostly at night, and in an age of expansion (although this author does not believe that had a long-term effect superceding population and international growth).

TRIVIA

Don Drysdale missed Sandy Koufax's perfect game. What did he say when told about it?

Answers to the trivia questions are on pages 178–179

But the old-timers often had to win low-scoring contests. Their fielders wore small gloves that made for errors. The fields they played on were rocky and bad bounces were more frequent.

In the 1965 World Series with Minnesota, Koufax did not pitch the opener because of Yom Kippur. After winning Game 5 in Los Angeles, Koufax was selected by Walt Alston to pitch Game 7 even though his earlier decision not to pitch the first game now meant he was going on two days' rest. It was Drysdale's turn on three days' rest. Alston was concerned about hurting Big D's pride, but Drysdale just told Alston, "If I was the manager, I'd pitch Sandy. I'll be ready. I'll go down to the bullpen and I'll be ready if something happens, but I'd pitch him too."

In those pre-ESPN days, televised baseball games were archaic by today's standards, but Koufax's Game 7 performance versus the Twins is occasionally shown on classic-sports stations. Watch it if you get the opportunity.

It was not Koufax's best game, which is oddly what makes it his best game. He dominated the Yankees more thoroughly in 1963, and of course his perfect game earlier that season is hard to top. Pitching on fumes in cold weather, Koufax faced a team of excellent hitters with power. Minnesota featured boppers like Harmon Killebrew, Tony Oliva, and Bob Allison, but rarely have such excellent hitters been made to look so bad.

Koufax broke most of the conventional pitching rules. He pitched "upstairs" all day in a manner few pitchers—Jim Palmer is one of the rare ones—ever get away with. He did not have his usually awesome curve, abandoning it when he continually failed to get any break off it early on. With the Twins knowing what was coming, and Koufax putting it in their wheelhouse all day, he just blew them away with pure power. As the game wound down, the Twins became more and more frustrated by their inability to catch up with him. The 2–0 score looked more like 12–0 from Minnesota's perspective.

At that moment, he was the greatest pitcher the game has ever seen.

Big D

Don Drysdale's place in the pantheon of pitching greatness is, like Koufax's, marred by several factors. Simply being considered the number two man behind Koufax and not the ace of the staff hurts him, although he *was* the staff ace from 1957 to 1962, and again from 1967–68. In '62 Koufax got off to an incredible start, but when he was injured it was Drysdale's 25-win, Cy Young Award–winning perform-ance that propelled the team to a 102–63 record. While Koufax was superb in his 1963 and 1965 World Series performances, Drysdale beat the Yankees 1–0 in '63 and stopped Minnesota's momentum flat in '65.

Another factor was his lack of run support. While Koufax often had to pitch with only a run or two behind him, the Dodgers seemed to give Drysdale even less. Finally, there is the longevity factor. Had he maintained his health and pitched another seven or eight years, Drysdale may well have gotten to 300 career wins, maybe more Cy Young Awards, and of course he would have been a part of some great Dodger teams. L.A. may well have won the 1969, 1971, and even 1973 National League West titles. What a treat it would have been to see Koufax versus the Mets' Tom Seaver and Drysdale versus Jerry Koosman in the '73 playoffs! With Drysdale pitching, even the '74 World Series may have gone a different direction.

Drysdale was "one of the finest competitors I have ever known," according to Duke Snider. "Don hated to lose—at anything. He didn't even like to hear the word lose."

Drysdale's on-field persona was as different from his actual per-sonality as any athlete. He was a tiger on the mound; mean and surly. Off the field he was a sweetheart, loved by all who knew him. He was extremely intelligent, too; a top student at Van Nuys High School whose teammate was Robert Redford and whose classmate was Natalie Wood. He turned down an academic scholarship to Stanford to take a bonus contract with the Brooklyn Dodgers and ascended to Ebbets Field in short order. While remembered for his Los Angeles exploits—he was *born* to be a Los Angeles Dodger—he was Brooklyn's best pitcher at the end.

He was a true fan favorite, the absolute epitome of what a major league pitcher looks like at 6'6", steely-eyed, never giving an inch. Drysdale worked inside without fear of repercussion, and in those days beanball wars between hard-throwers in the National League—

When Don Drysdale and Sandy Koufax held out for larger contracts in 1966, they claimed they had acting careers to fall back on. Drysdale looked good in Western attire, but neither he nor Koufax was confused with Olivier.

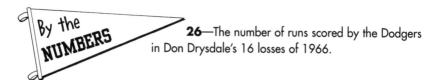

26—The number of runs scored by the Dodgers in Don Drysdale's 16 losses of 1966.

Gibson, Seaver, Jim Maloney, et al—were legendary. Drysdale never had a designated hitter to protect him and in fact was one of the game's greatest hitting pitchers. He easily could have forged a big-league career playing first base. He was cat-quick, fielded his position beautifully, had a great pickoff move, and was probably the best athlete in the Dodgers' Los Angeles history. Whether Drysdale hit batters on purpose has been disputed.

"Drysdale had the reputation of being a headhunter, which is an exaggeration," was Snider's assessment. "Well, maybe only a slight exaggeration. Don wasn't always trying to hit batters, but he didn't hesitate to throw inside, which a pitcher has to do to be successful, and he didn't mind capitalizing on his reputation to get an edge."

Drysdale approached Mickey Mantle before a 1963 World Series game at Dodger Stadium and asked him, "Well, Mick, where would you like one today?"

When Alston told him to walk Frank Robinson, who was just as competitive and crowded the plate like a subway masher, Drysdale figured it was the perfect chance to gain a psychological edge. After hitting F. Robby, Drysdale said, "I figured, why waste three pitches?"

Drysdale led the senior circuit in hit batsmen five times, and he was accused of doctoring the baseball. After his retirement he just said to the *L.A. Times,* "Sure I hit guys," and smiled when the subject of Vaseline balls came up. He wanted every edge he could get, and considering he usually had a run or two to work with, he needed it.

But Drysdale was talent personified. He threw well over 90 mph, not as fast as Koufax, but *harder.* Catcher John Roseboro said that Koufax, who could bring it around 100 mph, threw a "light" fastball; a rise that had more speed but because of trajectory landed perfectly in his glove.

Drysdale, on the other hand, threw a hard, naturally sinking fastball, which burned Roseboro's hand as it exploded into his glove. This also made for broken bats, double-play grounders, jammed thumbs, stinging hands...or worse. While he made use of the Brylcreem on his

That in 1966 spring holdouts caused great angst with the Dodgers? Buzzie Bavasi threatened to "blackball" Maury Wills if he did not sign a $75,000 contract, but he later was banished to Pittsburgh anyway. When Koufax and Drysdale held out, they told Bavasi they were "independently wealthy" and did not need baseball, to which the GM wished them "good luck." They made a movie, Warning Shot, with David Janssen. Koufax took a $110,000 advance to write his autobiography. Big D seriously considered an acting career or an offer from a Japanese clubs. They both signed, but the events were a precursor to labor troubles of the next decades.

well-coifed hair, making the baseball go dipsy-doodle, his natural sinking action could easily be mistaken for an illegally enhanced pitch. Drysdale was a workhorse who always pitched over 300 innings per season, had to be removed from games at the point of a gun (despite having Perranoski and Phil Regan in the bullpen), and tossed an incredible 49 career shutouts. He never missed a start, which makes his early retirement so maddening because he looked indestructible.

Drysdale also had a lot to do with Koufax's popularity. Drysdale befriended the shy Koufax. He showed the young New Yorker the sights when the team came out West, and they became connected to each other both on and off the field. In 1966, they teamed up in a "joint holdout," looking for three-year contracts totaling $1.05 million, to be divided equally. The Dodgers held the line, and Drysdale ended up signing a one-year deal for $110,000 (Sandy got a little more). Whether that holdout caused him to go 13–16 in 1966 is up for debate. His ERA was over 3.00 for the first time in years, but he was also hindered by more notoriously poor offensive support.

In the 1966 World Series, Drysdale pitched well, but the Oriole staff stopped L.A.'s bats cold. Jim Palmer beat Koufax, and in Game 4 at Memorial Stadium, Dave McNally bested Big D, 1–0.

Drysdale became an announcer and was part of the California Angels' broadcast team when Nolan Ryan broke Koufax's single-season strikeout record, garnering 383 in 1973. Later he teamed with Vin Scully and Ross Porter on Dodger broadcasts, but suffered an untimely heart attack in 1993, passing away at an early age.

"The Year of the Pitcher"

After Koufax retired in the fall of 1966, little was expected of the Dodgers, and that was what they delivered. They were mediocre in 1967 and not much better in 1968. In 1969 they contended in the "Wild, Wild West," the new division format that was exciting because, while the New York Mets (amazingly) won 100 games to take the East, the Braves, Giants, Reds, Dodgers, and even the Astros, battled it out for the 93 wins needed to win the West.

America, the city of Los Angeles, baseball—the times they were a-changin', as the song went. The Dodgers, so much a part of baseball's past, failed on and off the field to meet the requirements of change. They were old school. Even when Dr. Martin Luther King Jr. was assassinated in 1968, the team of Jackie Robinson held out until public opinion was so heavy against them that there was no choice but to cancel a game scheduled the night of his funeral.

But there was one major highlight. That was Don Drysdale's extraordinary six consecutive shutouts and 58⅔ scoreless innings streak of 1968. It was Drysdale's "last hurrah," although he did not know it at the time. Not yet 32 years of age, it seemed that Big D had emerged from Koufax's shadow to establish himself as L.A.'s all-time ace pitcher. The rugged Drysdale could attain all the career records that Koufax was prevented from winning due to injuries.

But Drysdale's sidewinding, twisting pitching motion put a lot of strain on his arm. He came down with the curiously named "tennis elbow" injury in 1969, calling it quits.

Nobody in the American or National League could hit the baseball worth a lick. It was the "Year of the Pitcher."

That by 1969 Walter O'Malley was the most powerful owner in baseball, reputed to have personally chosen Bowie Kuhn as the commissioner of baseball? O'Malley, not Kuhn, had the greatest influence on the game over the next years. It was his hard-line stance on the fledgling Player's Union and free agency that created conditions leading to major strikes in 1972, 1981, and eventually 1994.

It was as if Koufax and Drysdale had so dominated the hitters throughout the decade that everybody forgot how to swing the bat. The combined earned run average of 20 major league teams in both leagues was below 3.00. The All-Star Game was a 1–0 affair (National League). The American League batting champion, Carl Yastrzemski, was the only .300 hitter in that league at .301. Detroit's Mickey Lolich won three World Series games to earn the MVP award. The MVPs of both leagues were pitchers. In the AL, it was 31-game winner Denny McLain, the first to achieve that magic number of wins since 1934 and, to this day, the last to do it. The NL winner was Bob Gibson who, despite winning *only* 22, had a better year than McLain.

Gibby threw 13 shutouts and had a scoreless inning streak of 48 straight innings. His ERA, 1.12, is by far the greatest in baseball history, a record that may stand forever. In the World Series, he was even better in his first two victories than Koufax had been in previous Series games, if that is possible. In Game 1 he broke Sandy's Series strikeout record when 17 Tigers went down. Still dominating in a 0–0 Game 7 duel with Lolich, bad defense betrayed him and he was finally beaten.

But as great as Gibson, McLain, and a host of other 20-game winners, strikeout specialists, no-hit, even perfect game pitchers and microscopic ERA artists were in '68, it was Drysdale who captivated the baseball world at a time, frankly, when the world needed a distraction from reality.

But as great as Drysdale was in 1968, there seemed to be another pitcher better, and that was whoever pitched against L.A., particularly Drysdale. The 1968 Dodgers were so pathetic at the plate as to make the '65 team look like the later Lumber Company in Pittsburgh, or Cincy's Big Red Machine. Drysdale just pitched with no runs time and again. After seven starts his lone win was a 1–0 decision over the lowly Mets. At that point, it was the only run scored by Los Angeles in its last four games.

Dan Hafner of the *Los Angeles Times* wrote that in order for Drysdale to win, he had to pitch shutouts, so that was what he did. The Cubs fell, 1–0. Asked if he had "20 shutouts" in him, Drysdale reiterated earlier comments that nobody should expect him to fill Koufax's shoes and that "I couldn't stand something like this every time out. I'm too old for that."

Koufax in his best season never had a run like Drysdale was embarking on. He tossed three more shutouts, setting his sights on the big-league record of five set by Doc White of the White Sox in another "year of the pitcher," 1904 (Waddell struck out 349, Jack Chesbro won 41).

Dodger Stadium was packed with 46,000 fans and L.A. actually led San Francisco 3–0 entering the ninth. Drysdale's fastball was fluky in its tailing movement, which led many to believe he threw spitballs. The first-place Giants would not go down easily. Willie McCovey walked and went to second on Jim Ray Hart's single. A walk loaded the bases with no outs. Alston would have removed Drysdale but he wanted the record to be broken. Nevertheless, he played the infield at double-play depth, conceding a run on a grounder.

Dick Dietz worked a 2–2 count. A wicked Drysdale sinker flew through the night sky, landing on his elbow, walking in the run to end the streak. But home-plate umpire Harry Wendelstedt said Dietz, halfway to first base, had made no effort to avoid the pitch, and under the rules it was called ball three. It is a rarely called rule, and suspicious under these circumstances, but Dietz's short fly to left was unable to score the slow McCovey from third.

Ty Cline's hard smash was fielded by Wes Parker, who threw home for the force out. Jack Hiatt popped to Parker. Drysdale had wiggled out of the jam, just as he had done in an earlier game with Houston. The

TRIVIA

What midseason trade ended over two years of Dodger doldrums, reviving the club and propelling them to contention in 1969?

Answers to the trivia questions are on pages 178–179

135

Giants were livid, accusing Drysdale of doctoring the ball and the umpire of pulling for the record. In a tight race they would eventually lose to St. Louis, San Francisco needed every win they could muster.

Drysdale then shut out Pittsburgh, 5–0. He was past Carl Hubbell's National League record and two behind the Major League record for consecutive scoreless innings (56) by Walter Johnson.

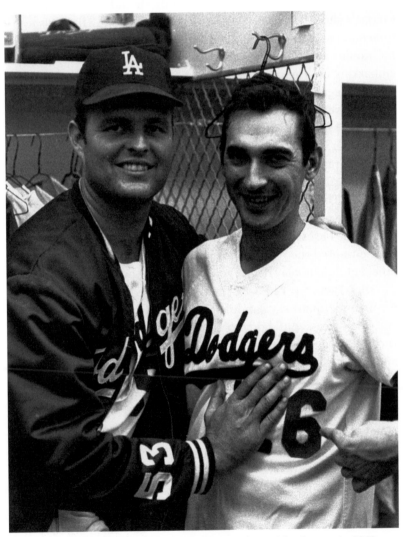

Don Drysdale with Paul Popovich after his sixth-straight shutout in 1968.

31—Willie Davis's 1969 hitting streak, breaking Zack Wheat's club record.

On June 8, 1968, Drysdale took the hill before a big crowd at Dodger Stadium, but it was different this time. Bobby Kennedy had been killed just a few days earlier and only a few miles away, at the Ambassador Hotel. Drysdale was a Kennedy admirer. He was shaky with his control, a Drysdale rarity, but pitched out of an early jam. Johnson's record fell when Drysdale got through the third, and he added two and two-thirds innings more before Howie Bedell's sacrifice fly scored Tony Taylor in the fifth to end it at 58⅔ innings.

Phillies manager Gene Mauch claimed Drysdale may have been inadvertently throwing a Vaseline ball. His hair was slicked with gel, and in touching his head he got the gel on his fingers, causing crazy things to happen. The umpire ordered him to keep his hands away from his cap or hair.

The Dodgers won 5–3. Drysdale's streak lifted them into second place, but after that both he and the team faltered. They finished in the second division.

Pride Goeth before the Fall

In 1974 the Los Angeles Dodgers got off to one of the best starts in many seasons. They appeared to be the culmination of years of sound farm system decisions, wise trades, and careful planning. The '74 Dodgers had all the earmarks of all-time greatness, but in the end their own hubris and lack of respect for the opposition brought them down.

The story begins in 1968. It was the beginning of an "out with the old, in with the new" mentality; a top-to-bottom plan. Peter O'Malley was beginning to assume greater control over the club from his father. Buzzie Bavasi put the wheels in motion, then handed the reins to Fresco Thompson. Eventually Al Campanis took over.

The "old Dodgers" like Don Drysdale were being replaced by a new crop of talent. It was felt that 1968 and possibly 1969 would be sacrificed to the future. Bavasi himself said after Koufax's departure that he did not think the fans expected much out of the club, which may have been a misreading of the front-running nature of the Southern California sports aficionado, accustomed by this time to Trojan and Bruin national championships, as well as Dodger titles. Frustration with the Lakers and Rams should have been a telling sign.

Tommy Lasorda, a one-time journeyman pitcher traded by Brooklyn to make room for Koufax, had devoted his life to the organization, first as a scout and now as a minor league manager. He directed the fortunes of the new Dodgers at Ogden and Spokane. Steve Garvey, Davey Lopes, Bill Russell, Ron Cey, Bill Buckner, Von Joshua, Bobby Valentine, Tom Paciorek, Joe Ferguson, Doyle Alexander, and Lee Lacy came along.

All-Time Sports Dynasties

1. Yankees—26 World Series wins
2. Montreal Canadiens—24 Stanley Cups
3. United States—medal leader in 17 Summer Olympic Games
4. Boston Celtics—16 NBA titles
5. USC—College World Series 12 times
6. Green Bay Packers—12 NFL titles
7. USC and Notre Dame—11 national championships each in football
8. Cardinals—10 World Series wins
9. A's—nine World Series wins
10. Dodgers—six World Series wins

Joining Wes Parker, Maury Wills (after exile to Pittsburgh), Willie Davis, Claude Osteen, Jim Lefebvre, and Don Sutton were talented youngsters like Ted Sizemore, Bill Sudakis, Willie Crawford, Tom Haller (by trade in 1969), Manny Mota, Len Gabrielson, Billy Grabarkewitz, Bill Singer, Jim Brewer, Sandy Vance, Pete Mikkelsen, Al Downing and Dick Allen (both by trade in 1971), Frank Robinson and Tommy John (both by trade in 1972).

The 1969–72 Dodgers were talented, entertaining, winning clubs. They contended in a five-team divisional race in '69, then gave San Francisco all they could handle before succumbing on the last day of the 1971 season. In 1970 and 1972 L.A. was competitive, but the Big Red Machine ran away with the division. By 1973 they had arrived. Throughout the summer the "Baby Blue" Dodgers threatened the established powerhouse Reds. Buckner and Steve Garvey split time at first base. The rest of the famed 1970s infield of Lopes, Russell, and Cey approached star quality. Sutton was an established pitcher, joined by former Angels ace Andy Messersmith. Osteen and John balanced a great staff. In the end, Cincinnati's 99 wins outlasted L.A.'s 95, but entering 1974 the Dodgers, having added ace reliever Mike Marshall and slugger Jimmy Wynn, were full of themselves.

When they broke out to a 17–6 April start, the team and their fans figured the division (and by acclamation the world championship) were locks. A 19–8 May gave them a 36–14 record versus the Reds' 27–19 mark. L.A. swept the Reds at home and away, then stayed strong at 16–10 in June. Entering a four-game showdown at Riverfront Stadium July 2–4, Los Angeles stood 52–24. The Reds were 44–31. When Cincinnati lost three out of four, it appeared to be all over but the shouting.

The similarities between 1951, 1962 (when the Dodgers blew it all), and other years, such as 1952 and 1963 (when the Dodgers got out to big leads but held on), did not register with this team or their supporters. To understand their mindset, one must consider the state of baseball, and indeed the country, in 1974.

Most teams were playing in dilapidated stadiums. The new stadiums, like Cincinnati's Riverfront, Philadelphia's Veteran's, and Pittsburgh's Three Rivers, were cookie-cutter monstrosities. The Dodgers' traditional rival, San Francisco, was horrible on the field and at the gate, playing in the abominable Candlestick. Attendance throughout baseball was down compared to L.A. Most teams wore brutal, garish uniforms with white or colored shoes. Players had hideous hairstyles, beards, and moustaches. Tradition was out. There were many great players, but the game seemed to have lost its sizzle to pro football. The Yankees were just another team. The country was in the throes of post-Vietnam/Watergate angst.

In the middle of this, the Dodgers in their traditional blue-and-whites, black shoes, modest haircuts, their perfect stadium filled every night, playing brilliantly, stood like a Colossus of Rhodes over Major League Baseball, at least in their own minds. The A's were two-time defending world champions, but their uniforms, long hair, poor fan support, and modest record in a weak division served to make the team look like a pale baseball imitation of L.A.'s grandeur.

Enter the Cincinnati Reds of Johnny Bench, Tony Perez, Joe Morgan, Pete Rose, and manager Sparky Anderson. This was the Big Red Machine that would win two straight world championships (1975–76). They featured future Hall of Famers, were proud, and not willing to quit. They were the one team in the National League that refused to be intimidated by Dodger panache. Cincinnati had improved after the July series with L.A., going 19–12 in July, while the Dodgers faltered a bit at 16–13. On August 5 they arrived for a nationally televised *Monday Night Baseball* game at Dodger Stadium having won four of five. It was their last gasp against a Dodger team that was hot again, riding a seven-game winning streak.

When Doug Rau beat Don Gullett, 6–3, and the teams were tied at 3–3 in the tenth inning the next evening, the season teetered on the brink for Cincy, but the Reds pulled out the extra-inning affair. Then they took the series the next night behind Jack Billingham over Andy Messersmith, 2–0. Getting shut out was a rude Dodger awakening. L.A. lost six straight in August while the Reds were hot.

After outlasting Cincinnati, the Dodgers thought beating the A's would be easy. Instead, Oakland taught them a lesson as they captured their third-straight world championship. Here, catcher Ray Fosse connects for a Game 5 homer off Don Sutton.

Down by 10½, Cincinnati had rallied to within one and a half before Sutton prevented a three-game Cincinnati sweep with a 7–1 September win. Like 1963 and 1952, but thankfully unlike 1951 and 1962, Los Angeles (102–60) recovered to win the division by four over the Reds (98–64). Mike Marshall won the Cy Young Award and Steve Garvey was the MVP.

In the playoffs, Los Angeles annihilated outgunned Pittsburgh. In the American League, Oakland beat Baltimore with pitching, but they seemed unimpressive doing it, just as they had in beating out the suspect Texas Rangers to capture their division.

When Oakland arrived at Dodger Stadium, it seemed like a joke. They looked like a softball team in their green-and-gold harlequin costumes with flowing, bad '70s hair. The Dodgers looked to be America's best and brightest. They were Hollywood's team and played it to the hilt. Beautiful starlets watched them adoringly. Only hardcore blue-collar fans ventured to the Oakland Coliseum.

Several Dodgers said nobody on the A's would even start for them. Oakland captain Sal Bando then suggested to outfielder Reggie Jackson, "Buck, I suggest we dispose of these people as quickly as possible."

"I couldn't agree more," said Jackson.

The A's did precisely as Bando suggested. Los Angeles thought they had beaten the best team in baseball—Cincinnati—forgetting that Oakland had beaten them in 1972, as well as a Met team that defeated the Reds in 1973. They seemed to forget the old adage that "pitching is 90 percent of the game," or "good pitching stops good hitting." Pick your cliché, but the Dodgers paid for their overconfidence.

Oakland's Ken Holtzman and the A's bullpen, with last-out help from Catfish Hunter, shut L.A. down 3–2 in the Dodger Stadium opener. Sutton held on for a 3–2 win in Game 2, but the Oakland swing was a nightmare. Mike Marshall arrogantly refused warm-ups after a toilet paper–throwing incident. Guessing fastball because of it, Joe Rudi smoked a first-pitch homer. Bill Buckner tried to stretch a single and error into three bases, committing the cardinal sin of making the first out at third base.

TRIVIA

What important trade did Los Angeles make prior to the 1965 season that helped them not only win two straight pennants, but also the 1974 N.L. Championship?

Answers to the trivia questions are on pages 178–179

Oakland pitching dominated. The Dodgers paid the price of respect, and like the Babylonians, Persians, Greeks, and Romans before them, "pride goeth before the fall." Los Angeles, who fell in five games, entered the offseason with their tails between their legs.

One Year at a Time

Walter Alston was a company man. After the tempestuous Leo Durocher and the egotistical Charlie Dressen, who insisted on a multi-year contract after the 1953 season, Alston was chosen to replace him. The message was clear: no multi-year deals. It took a certain kind of man to accept that premise, which Alston did year in and year out until 1976, when he called it quits on his own terms.

Alston was less than a marginal ballplayer, a rube in the eyes of many, especially in sophisticated New York. After his hiring, the *New York Daily News* ran the headline, "Walter Who?"

Alston came out of the University of Miami (Ohio) and managed in the Dodger farm system, but the team he inherited was so full of veterans that few had any association with him prior to 1954. He had played 13 minor league seasons, reaching the majors with the 1936 St. Louis Cardinals, only to strike out and return to the bushes from whence he never returned as a player.

He began to manage at Portsmouth of the Mid-Atlantic League, but when Branch Rickey took over the Dodgers, it was a break for Alston. Rickey had known him when he was the general manager at St. Louis. They had a lot in common; both were Midwesterners, very religious, and college men in an age in which the collegiate player was rare. Eventually, Alston took over Brooklyn's top farm club at Montreal.

Roy Campanella and Don Newcombe were not nearly as sophisticated as Jackie Robinson, and needed special care, which Alston gave them as they were making their way through the farm system. Junior Gilliam "loved" Alston, according to Duke Snider, and was made a coach under him, a fairly groundbreaking move at the time (which fulfilled a public wish made by Robinson at the 1972 World Series).

"And Walter flat-out bawled giving the eulogy at Gilliam's funeral in 1978," wrote Snider in *Few and Chosen: Defining Dodgers Greatness Across the Eras.* "It was the only time I ever saw Alston cry."

The problems between Robinson and Alston stemmed from an incident in which Robinson was injured. Alston continued to bench him. Robinson told the media he was ready to play. Alston did not like players taking internal conflicts to the media (although he used the media on more than one occasion) and confronted Robinson. A shouting match ensued.

Robinson may not have respected Alston at that point. Alston had not earned his spurs, but despite his quiet demeanor he had a temper and was tough. A fight was averted only when players intervened. On another occasion, Robinson got in an argument with the

Walt Alston managed with one-year contracts from 1954 to 1976. Here he relaxes after beating the Yankees in a 1956 World Series game. New York eventually captured the Series.

That of all the young Dodger stars who came through the organization in the late 1960s and early 1970s, Bobby Valentine was considered the best? A favorite of Tom Lasorda, he was packaged along with Frank Robinson and Bill Singer in a key trade with California for Andy Messersmith prior to the 1973 campaign. Messersmith was a star for the Dodgers. When Valentine's spikes got caught in a seam on the outfield fence, similar to Pete Reiser, the injury for all practical purposes destroyed his career. He became the manager of the Mets and Rangers, as well as a Japanese club.

umpire but Alston never came to his defense, which is the traditional role of managers when players get into it with the umpire. The tough feelings remained.

Alston took over a team in 1954 that had won two straight National League pennants, had lost on the last day twice before that, and had won two of three league titles before that. When his team fell to the hated New York Giants (Willie Mays having returned from the army) with a veteran squad, all at the height of their careers, blame fell on him.

"With a year under his belt, Alston became a better manager," said Snider. In Los Angeles, Alston proved his worth. He had his ups and downs, but the Dodgers of the mid-1960s were a major challenge for any manager. True, he had the best pitching staff in the game, but he used it wisely. He manufactured runs by playing "small ball," making use of his player's speed and intelligence. He bunted, used the hit-and-run, knew how to get runs without base hits, and most certainly without home runs.

He signed 23 one-year contracts, won seven pennants and four world championships. He had his problems with veterans, and later with Koufax, but he was Sandy's only manager and the results are hard to argue with. His handling of the younger Dodgers who came up in the 1960s and 1970s was superb. But his greatest challenge was imposed on him by the club itself.

In 1963 famed Los Angeles sportswriter Melvin Durslag penned "Manager with a Hair Shirt," an excellent look at Alston's travails fending off the encroachment of Leo Durocher, for *Look* magazine.

The article detailed Alston's run-in with Koufax and pitcher Larry Sherry, whom he discovered coming in late after curfew. Alston became so enraged that he banged their locked door down, breaking his World Series ring. Alston was a lit fuse. He was quiet and reserved, taking the abuse and lack of respect of his team, the brass, and the media, but would eventually explode. When that happened, he was ornery.

In L.A. Alston was frustrated at how many over-the-hill veterans from Brooklyn were kept on the roster against his wishes. He knew the team needed to go with young blood if they were to compete, but when the team faltered in 1958 despite his protestations, it was Alston who was universally blamed. Charlie Dressen was brought back as a coach, immediately infusing speculation that he would take over the club.

When Alston's youth movement was allowed to pay dividends in the form of the 1959 world championship, it earned him little leeway. Dressen was let go and Alston might have had some breathing space. But Durocher was being effectively blackballed from baseball and approached Durslag to write a favorable article on his behalf. With the expansion Angels moving into L.A. in 1961 and the club scheduled to open Dodger Stadium in 1962, Walter O'Malley decided to create excitement in order to counter the Angels. L.A. hired Durocher.

"Though Alston had nothing to do with Leo's appointment, he was solicited to make the official announcement," wrote Durslag. "After a flight from Darrtown to California, he had the privilege of revealing to the world the newest candidate for his job."

Durslag pointed out the obvious differences between the two. Alston lived in a "comfortable but modest home." His hobby was woodworking. Leo lived in a $150,000 Trousdale Estates mansion. Alston drove a Mercury, Leo a Caddy. Alston's clothes came off the rack from a store in Ohio. An exclusive Hollywood tailor designed Durocher's. Alston preferred to "carry a beef" to the next day, when

TRIVIA

What Dodger pitcher grooved Hank Aaron's 715th career home run at Atlanta in 1974?

Answers to the trivia questions are on pages 178–179

147

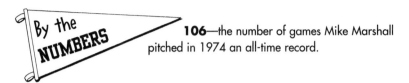

106—the number of games Mike Marshall pitched in 1974 an all-time record.

cooler heads prevailed, while Durocher preferred to handle disputes in the here and now.

Between 1961 and 1964, the Dodger front office constantly backed away from endorsing Alston. Buzzie Bavasi said finishing second to Cincinnati in 1961 was "no disgrace," leading to the next question: would Alston return?

"I didn't say that," said Bavasi. Alston just twisted in the wind the whole time Durocher was around. After the 1962 disaster, it was all-out war. Public "votes of confidence" for Alston served only to have the opposite effect. His job was always a day, or a bad game away from being lost.

"The Dodgers never plan to fire Alston," said one observer. "They prefer to torment him."

When Durslag rebuked Alston in print over a dugout berating of Durocher, Walter confronted the writer and snapped, "You're pretty sensitive about Durocher's feelings, but you don't seem to care much about mine."

Alston demonstrated some thin skin on this and other occasions. The strange Kabuki theatre with Leo lasted through '64. Alston was retained after 1962, probably because attendance was so outstanding that the team did not want to tinker with gate success. Bavasi realized he did not need Hollywood players (like Durocher) in order to entertain Hollywood. After winning the 1963 World Series, Alston finally had his respect. After Durocher was let go a year later (eventually taking over the Chicago Cubs), Alston finally had his team.

Rematch

The Cincinnati Reds dominated baseball in 1975 and 1976. History judges this to be one of the great short-term dynasties ever. The A's, split by free agency, faded toward eventual oblivion. The Dodgers, just as they had been from 1969–73, were competitive, entertaining, and successful at the gate, but never sniffed Cincinnati.

The Reds looked to be dominant again in 1977. When they traded for Tom Seaver of the Mets, they were expected to win 105 games or more. Seaver, with the run support he never had in New York, was considered the best bet to be the first 30-game-winner since Denny McLain.

But the Dodgers were a veteran ballclub with all the pieces of the puzzle by 1977. Messersmith was lost to free agency but Tommy John won 20, while Sutton, Burt Hooton, Rick Rhoden, and Doug Rau rounded out one of the best pitching staffs in the game.

The infield of first baseman Steve Garvey (33 homers, 115 RBIs), second baseman Davey Lopes, third baseman Ron Cey (30 homers), and shortstop Bill Russell was solidly in place. Steve Yeager, a defensive star, had replaced Joe Ferguson behind the plate. Homegrown Reggie Smith from Compton Centennial High hit 32 homers. Dusty Baker, acquired from Atlanta, hit 30. With the fences brought in at Dodger Stadium, L.A. had the new look of a power-hitting team with four 30-home-run hitters. Santa Monica's Rick Monday, already a fan favorite when as a member of the Cubs he saved the American flag from protestors trying to torch it on the Dodger Stadium field in 1976, came over via trade to play center.

But the sense that this year was the season in which Los Angeles would derail the Big Red Machine came in the person of Tommy

Lasorda. He had risen from pitcher to scout to winter league skipper to minor league manager to third-base coach, where he embodied Dodger arrogance in 1974. Wearing a microphone, he was captured on now well-worn footage telling American League umpire Ron Luciano that the senior circuit was superior, just as Oakland was proving him wrong.

Alston finally retired in 1976. Lasorda's hiring was a given. He filled the air with enthusiasm at Vero Beach with his love of the Dodgers. He worshipped the organization and was an ambassador for the team and the game. While overwrought in many ways, Lasorda helped bring back baseball's popularity.

1977 was eerily similar to 1974, with Los Angeles getting off to one of the all-time great starts (17–3 in May, 22 out of the first 26). They played consistently, overcame a 14–15 August, and finished at 98–64.

The Reds, 9–10 in April, got hot in June. When they acquired Seaver, who threw a brilliant shutout in his first Cincinnati appearance, all bets were off, however. The Reds' great lineup from 1975–76 was still in place, veteran but not old. They were thought to have improved with George Foster's emergence as a star. Curiously, this offensive juggernaut failed to support Seaver, who despite posting a 21–6 mark (14–3 as a Red) could have carried his team to the pennant and that 30-win campaign had they scored for him. At 88 wins, Cincinnati's championship run never materialized.

The Dodgers drew 2,955,087 fans—an all-time record. The concept of drawing three or even four million fans now seemed plausible. Overall baseball attendance improved. The Dodgers did not have the arrogance of 1974, when they felt that they were superior in all ways, although the Giants were a joke in '77 and there was no semblance of rivalry, at least in the minds of fans south of Big Sur.

DID YOU KNOW . . . That Tommy Lasorda "...as a player and manager in the Puerto Rican, Cuban, Panamanian, Dominican Republic, and Venezuelan winter leagues, incited more Latin American brawls than anyone since Che Guevara," wrote Larry Keith in *Sports Illustrated*?

Ron Cey is greeted by Dusty Baker and Davey Lopes after a home run versus the Yankees in the 1978 World Series.

A tough Phillie club, featuring Cy Young winner Steve Carlton and Hall of Fame third baseman Mike Schmidt, gave them all they could handle, but fell in four National League Championship Series games. The reason L.A. was not overconfident as in the past loomed large in the form of their World Series opponents, the New York Yankees.

George Steinbrenner had taken advantage of the new economics of the game, returning the Bronx Bombers to glory. They had made it to the World Series in 1976 and were managed by the tempestuous, popular New York icon, Billy Martin. Superstar Reggie Jackson, one of Oakland's "Dodger killers" three years earlier, had not missed a step.

The Dodgers had nothing on New York, but they were confident that they had the power and the pitching to knock the Yankees back, just as they had done in 1963. But there was no Sandy Koufax or Don Drysdale. Furthermore, their bullpen was suspect.

Don Sutton pitched well in the opener, but it was not enough. The tone for the Series was set in a 4–3 extra-inning New York win. The

By the NUMBERS

87–42—Tommy John's sterling record as a Dodger. After missing an entire season, doctors successfully performed what came to be called "Tommy John surgery" on his left arm. He came back to be the 1976 National League Comeback Player of the Year, a 20-game-winner in L.A., and a 20-game-winner for the Yankees after signing with them as a free agent.

Dodgers could not shut the door on the Yankees. Down three games to one, Sutton pitched Los Angeles to a 10–4 win, and Steve Garvey expressed optimism that Dodger pitching could hold New York at Yankee Stadium. Instead, Jackson hit three home runs in Game 6 (five total home runs in the Series) to power the Bombers to a six-game world championship victory that was never in any real doubt.

The 1978 season was a different story with the same ending. When the Dodgers and Reds both got off to 4–0 starts, the season had all the earmarks of a classic confrontation between the two great National League rivals of the decade, but both clubs tailed off. Out of the blue, the Giants came on strong, putting on an offensive display at Dodger Stadium to serve notice, then forging a six-game lead by midsummer.

The Dodgers had a hard time taking San Francisco seriously. They had been a joke for years and changed their uniforms to a garish scheme typical of the era. But attrition, the old ally of quality in a long baseball season, won out in the end. Vida Blue faltered and the aging Willie McCovey could only hit so many clutch homers. Cincinnati's age was now apparent, and the team gave 16-game-winner Seaver no support. Sparky Anderson's team was strong enough to make a race of it, but in the end L.A. (95–67) outlasted the Reds (92–69) and the Giants (89–73).

The Dodgers were less spectacular than in '77. Garvey hit 21 homers and drove in 113. Baker fell to 11 homers. Davey Lopes's speed was reminiscent of Maury Wills. The pitching was excellent, but not Koufax-Drysdale great. Baseball, spurred by winners in the two most important markets, was on the rebound in 1978, with L.A. leading the charge past 3 million at the gate. It was a big year in L.A., in many ways the culmination of the greatest "golden age" in the Golden State's sports history.

Los Angeles took care of the Phillies again in the National League Championship Series, but the Yankees loomed larger than life in a World Series rematch. L.A. had little swagger left after humbling defeats at the hands of the A's (1974), Reds (1975–76), and Yankees (1977). That said, they were still *the Dodgers!*

TRIVIA

What is Tommy Lasorda's name for God?

Answers to the trivia questions are on pages 178–179

New York was as hot a team as anybody could remember, having come back from Billy Martin's resignation and a 14-game deficit on July 17 to break Boston's hearts before dispatching Kansas City in the playoffs. But the tables seemed turned when L.A. took advantage of shaky Yankee pitching to win Game 1, 11–5, followed by Bob Welch's clutch strikeout of Reggie Jackson in Game 2 to win 4–3 going back to New York.

Ron Guidry was for that one season as good as any pitcher in history, but he needed Graig Nettles's heroics to take the 5–1 Game 3 win. When the Dodgers led 3–0 the next day, they were almost there. Instead, Reggie Jackson stuck his hip into a thrown ball in a pickle, deflecting it and costing Los Angeles the 4–3 loss. The air was out of the tire. New York then trounced them at Yankee Stadium. Behind Reggie Jackson's homer and Catfish Hunter's pitching in L.A., it was another Yankee title, 7–2. For the Dodgers, it was "wait till next year" again. Getting handled by Hunter and Jackson was a further humiliating reminder of what the A's had done to them four years earlier.

On a personal note, this author was in the stands for that disappointing Game 6 loss. I had tickets to the Game 7 that never was played. It was bad enough that I was unable to see the seventh game, but the ticket was in my game program and I forgot about it. Sometime in November I glanced at the program and saw the ticket. The expiration date for getting a refund of my money was the previous day.

Garv

Steve Garvey was one of those guys who was "born to be a Dodger." His father was the club's bus driver during spring training in Vero Beach, Florida. Garvey grew up in Tampa, spending much of his time around the club during camp.

He went to Michigan State University, where he was part of Duffy Daugherty's great football program. In 1966 the Spartans tied Notre Dame, 10–10, in the "game of the century" at East Lansing.

Garvey came up under the tutelage of minor league manager Tom Lasorda, breaking into the big leagues in 1969, but not truly securing his job until 1974. He was considered a third baseman. He appeared in 115 games in 1970 and 1971, slowly but surely separating himself from the pack of young Dodger studs—Grabarkewitz, Sudakis, Sizemore, Buckner, Paciorek.

In the winter of 1971–72, the Dodgers traded first baseman Dick Allen, a powerful hitter considered a troublemaker by the conservative O'Malleys, to Chicago for Tommy John. It would spur the team to greatness and make the first baseman's position wide open.

John was a sinkerball pitcher, as was most of the staff. These were not the strikeout artists of the Koufax heyday. They produced a lot of grounders, making for a lot of throws to first base. It was essential that whoever played that position be capable of scooping errant tosses. Garvey was that man, but only after failing at third base.

"When I got to the Dodgers in 1972," said John in *Few and Chosen: Defining Dodgers Greatness Across the Eras* by Duke Snider with Phil Pepe, "their infield was Wes Parker at first, Jim Lefebvre at second, Maury Wills at short, and Steve Garvey at third. Garvey was horrible at third base. He could field the ball, field shots, but he couldn't throw it across the infield. If it hadn't been for Parker, Garvey would have had 100 errors."

Garvey made 28 errors at third in 85 games. John, the consummate groundball pitcher, paid the biggest price, winning a mere 11 games in the prime of his career.

"Toward the end of the season," said John, "they gave Garv a first baseman's glove. Parker had announced his retirement and everybody thought Bill Buckner or Tom Paciorek was going to get the

Steve Garvey was born to be a Dodger. His father drove the club's spring training bus in Florida. Garvey signed with scout Tom Lasorda after starring in baseball and football at Michigan State.

Position	Name
Pitcher	Don Sutton
Pitcher	Andy Messersmith
Pitcher	Tommy John
Pitcher	Claude Osteen
Relief Pitcher	Mike Marshall
Catcher	Steve Yeager
First Baseman	Steve Garvey
Second Baseman	Davey Lopes
Third Baseman	Ron Cey
Shortstop	Bill Russell
Outfielder	Bill Buckner
Outfielder	Dusty Baker
Outfielder	Reggie Smith
Manager	Tommy Lasorda

first-base job, but they gave Garvey a first baseman's glove and said, 'Take it over because we have a kid down at Triple A ball who can play third.' That was Ron Cey.

"Garv made himself into a pretty good first baseman."

In his first year at his new position, Garvey made only five errors in 76 games. He hit .304 with eight homers and 50 RBIs. John, with good defense behind him, upgraded to 16 wins.

John went on to win 60 games over five seasons with the famed Garvey-Lopes-Russell-Cey infield behind him. Garvey hit .297 during that stretch, driving in 95 or more runs four times. Nevertheless, as late as 1973 he was still battling for the first baseman's position with Bill Buckner. It really was not until 1974, when Garvey won the Most Valuable Player award, that he earned the position once and for all over the star-crossed Buckner, a truly excellent player.

He was the strong, silent type, much like his boyhood hero, Gil Hodges. Garv could handle the low throw as well as any first baseman in the league. Offensively, Garvey was a total clutch hitter. The difference between Garvey and later Dodger first baseman Eric

Karros was in their respective abilities to come through with the game on the line. Karros's statistics rivaled Garvey's, but his value to the team did not.

TRIVIA

What were the first three Dodger numbers to be formally retired?

Answers to the trivia questions are on pages 178–179

During the decade-long run that marked Garvey's greatest years, the Dodgers captured four National League championships, never lost in the playoffs, and won one World Series (as opposed to the "Karros era," in which L.A. never won a single postseason game). Garvey slammed more than 20 home runs five times, drove in 100 runs five times, and batted over .300 seven times. Aside from winning the MVP award in 1974, he earned MVP honors in that year's All-Star Game after having been voted the starting first baseman by write-in balloting. That season he hit 21 homers, drove in 111 runs, and batted .312. When Los Angeles played Oakland in the World Series, Davey Lopes, Ron Cey, and others popped off, giving the A's little respect, but Garvey kept his mouth shut. He performed well against Oakland, but it was not enough.

Garvey was a hero figure in L.A. A good Irish Catholic boy, he was a poster child for all-American clean living. He had a beautiful blonde wife and an adorable family. He spoke about some day pursuing Republican politics, making the point that, "I have to start at the Senate." His righteous ways roiled some of the more free-spirited Dodgers, namely Don Sutton and Ron Cey. There were spats and disputes, but he remained a fan favorite.

Garvey's last year, 1982, was a tearful event for Dodger fans, who could not believe the club would let go of such an icon in favor of Mike Marshall. Garvey just went to San Diego and helped the 1984 Padres make it to the World Series.

In his later years, Garvey's great image was despoiled when he fathered several children out of wedlock. His wife left him and told tales out of school that were both disparaging and embarrassing. His political aspirations dried up, and even his ability to make a living through the media that seemed such a natural for the soft-spoken, intelligent Garvey, never really materialized.

Fernandomania

The year 1981 was a lousy, rotten year. It started out as one of the best seasons in baseball history. The game was now thoroughly revived after years of lackluster attendance. In Oakland, new owner-ship totally revitalized the A's franchise. The once second-rate Angels were a thriving organization in Orange County. The Dodgers got off to a big start behind rookie sensation Fernando "El Toro" Valenzuela, a Mexican import who had the town—Latinos, whites, blacks, everybody—gaga over the Dodgers. It promised to be a record-breaking season on the field and at the gate.

But by 1981 free agency and the baseball union was a cancer that had metastasized to the point where it was all but inoperable. A season of wonder and joy was split apart by a horrid strike. It is a testament to the pure greatness of the game—not to the players or any one team—that even though the players have greedily struck on numerous occasions, they cannot destroy the game. But they destroyed 1981.

Officially, it was the year of "Fernandomania," a season in which the team bathed itself in glory by beating the Yankees to win the World Series, but it is all one big asterisk (*strike season). In a game of stats that mean nothing unless compared with the time-honored 162-game template, 1981 was reduced to a season in which L.A.'s 63–47 record just sat there. A nice record through 110 games with 52 left, and as anybody who knows anything about 1951 or 1962 understands, there is still a lot of baseball to be played in those last 52 contests!

A record of 63–47 certainly does not shout "that championship season"—unless one is talking about the rookie league—especially since Cincinnati finished 66–42, but failed to make the so-called

Colorful southpaw Fernando Valenzuela in 1981 World Series action against the New York Yankees. Photo courtesy of Getty Images.

playoffs because they were not the so-called champions of either the "first half" or "second half" of the "season." What a joke!

The fans have the right to be bitter because they were denied so much. For baseball purists who root for the Dodgers, it is all so insubstantial. Officially, they are the World Champions of 1981, but the reality is that this "title" is bathed in that strike-shortened asterisk.

All of that said, Fernando was magic and deserves his kudos. Valenzuela had won two games in September/October 1980. He was still officially a rookie, pressed into the opening day start of 1981 because of an injury to the scheduled starter. He responded with a shutout and won his first eight straight. Others have won eight straight games, but few as brilliantly as Fernando's start.

Vida Blue of Oakland had gotten off to a similar start in 1971 at 10–1, but Valenzuela was not a power pitcher like Blue. He was pudgy and looked to be older than the press guide said he was (21, but he probably was older). He had perfect control, mound moxie, and a fabulous screwball that broke away from left-handed hitters. Nobody knew much about him, so the scouting reports were of little use. Besides, he was so mysterious that hitters knew what was coming (the screwball) but could not hit him.

Nicknamed "el Toro" ("the Bull"), Valenzuela launched L.A. to a blazing fast start, igniting baseball fever in the Latino neighborhoods. The Dodgers, despite being the team of Jackie Robinson, were a very conservative organization catering to an upscale suburban fan base, who ironically would drive from all points north, south, east, and west right through the barrio neighborhoods surrounding Dodger Stadium. They would park in their color-coded spots, watch the games, leave early to beat the traffic, and spend little or no money in the community.

If Dodger Stadium has any drawbacks, it is the lack of a surrounding business community of restaurants, bars, shops, and nightlife, such as the one that evolved after the building of San

Francisco's Pac Bell Park (now AT&T Park) in 2000.

But the Dodgers always held their ticket prices down. Baseball games were the last refuge of cost-conscious entertainment for the working man. Latino families could purchase six pavilion seats and have a blast watching their heroes—especially Fernando—light up the sky.

TRIVIA

What did former player and broadcaster Joe Garagiola say about Tommy Lasorda?

Answers to the trivia questions are on pages 178–179

The magic that was 1981 came screeching to a halt when, in June, the players struck. It was stupidity and greed beyond comprehension. Curt Flood's Supreme Court case decided in 1972, although denied, opened the door to free agency. By the late 1970s, salaries were skyrocketing. There were no more "poor" ballplayers scratching for a living, selling insurance, or working as bartenders in the offseason. To strike in 1981 was to try and "kill the golden goose," and as mentioned, only because Americans love their baseball so much did the game survive the carnage.

The details are too dreary to recount. In August they started playing again. L.A. lost its edge during the layoff. Fernando was average in the second half. Had they not struck, he and the team may well have put together memorable numbers (100 wins for the team, 20 for Fernando). Instead, Fernando's 13–7 mark merely *exists* in the record books.

He won the Cy Young Award, which rightfully should have gone to Cincinnati's Tom Seaver (14–2), and for added measure earned the MVP on top of the Rookie of the Year trophy.

The playoffs, which featured an extra "Divisional Series" (before the one instituted with the creation of an extra division and series playoffs in 1994), were at least entertaining. L.A. beat Houston, the "second half" champ, then took on Montreal. A famed Rick Monday homer in a light snowfall gave them the National League pennant, putting them in the World Series versus the Yankees, with Jackson and Dave Winfield.

When New York went up two games to none, Dodger fans could console themselves by saying it was just an asterisk season, so winning the 1981 World Series would not carry great meaning. When they came storming back, they had to find great meaning.

Fernando helped with a 131-pitch complete-game 5–4 victory in Game 3 at Dodger Stadium. It was a game that nobody would complete in today's pitch-count era. It was a game that showed why Valenzuela was a bit of a one-shot wonder (his screwball was no longer a mystery; he was hit around and far from dominant) while at the same time demonstrating why he succeeded (he was a total bulldog).

George Steinbrenner began to complain, the Yankees pressed and lost their edge. L.A. then pulled out an 8–7 win, followed by a Jerry Reuss gem, 2–1, over Ron Guidry. In New York the momentum was impossible to quell as the Dodger hit parade spurred a 9–2 victory, with star-crossed reliever Steve Howe closing it out for a six-game world championship.

The Last Hurrah

The Los Angeles Dodgers received a real shot in the arm when hard-hitting outfielder Kirk Gibson signed a free-agent contract prior to the 1988 season. Gibson hit 25 homers and drove in 76 runs that summer, stats that pale in comparison to today's sluggers, but it was Gibson's team that went all the way. Gibson *hated* to lose: he played in pain, he played hard every inning of every game, and he saw to it that his teammates did, too. A look at the Dodgers' offensive numbers begs the question: how did these guys finish in first place? The answer can be summarized in the words of the late, great Connie Mack, who once said, "pitching is 90 percent of the game."

Dodger tradition was carried on by a corps of hard-throwing horses who gave them a lot of innings. Tim Belcher brought high heat, going 12–6 with a 2.91 ERA. Tim Leary finished 17–11, also with a 2.91 ERA.

With all due respect for Gibson, who won the award, the Most Valuable Player in the National League that year was pitcher Orel Hershiser. A fine pitcher over his career, explaining exactly what got into him *that* year is surely beyond this author's expertise. He had one of those "mystery seasons," like Dean Chance in 1964, or Ron Guidry in 1978; guys with solid ability who for one year are absolutely untouchable.

That was Orel. By midseason he was having a good year, but Cincinnati left-hander Danny Jackson was the frontrunner for the Cy Young Award. Then Hershiser started throwing shutouts. A biomechanics expert might point to finger pressure, release point, the muscles and tendons in his right arm, but whatever it was, you cannot bottle it. The baseballs Hershiser threw had extraordinary

In 1988 Orel Hershiser got in a groove like none before or since. He threw 59 straight scoreless innings and pitched L.A. to a World Series win over the vaunted Oakland A's.

spin; delivered three-quarter arm, his pitches created a terrific sinking action so that wood bats meeting one of his natural sinkers seemingly had the effect of meeting up with a shot-put. Hershiser would throw a sinker to a right-handed hitter that would break in with the same kind of force as a slider from a southpaw like Steve Carlton. The utterly unexplainable aspect of it all was that no matter how much movement the ball had, Hershiser could throw it for pinpoint corner strikes in such ways as to make pitching seem like the easiest activity in the world.

For the last two months of the regular season it went on like that, and when it was over, Hershiser had thrown 59 straight scoreless innings, breaking Don Drysdale's major league record. If anybody had any doubt that Hershiser and his club were a team of destiny, Orel's final start at San Diego would remove all questions. He needed 10 innings for the record, so it appeared that he would have to pitch a shutout, then wait until 1989 to break the mark. Naturally, after nine innings, the score was conveniently tied at 0–0, allowing Hershiser to pitch a scoreless tenth, breaking the record en route to a 23–8 record and the Cy Young Award.

The 94-67 Dodgers hosted the 100-victory Mets in the Championship Series opener, and the New Yorkers were already talking about playing the vaunted Oakland A's in the World Series. For eight innings, Hershiser's sinker was *insane*. He could knock the eyelash off a fly at 60 feet, six inches, and led 2–0. In the ninth, New York scored three times against Hershiser and reliever Jay Howell and won it. If ever a team should have been mentally beaten, it was the Dodgers, but the Blue Crew won Game 2. Hershiser started the third game, left leading in the seventh, but again the bullpen blew it. In a pivotal Game 4, Mike Scioscia belted a two-run game-tying homer off Dwight Gooden at Shea Stadium, followed by Gibson's twelfth-inning blast to win it, 5–4. Series MVP Hershiser was as good as good can be in the 6–0 Game 7 clincher at Dodger Stadium. Few pitchers have so dominated good hitters in such important games: Sandy Koufax versus the Twins in '65, Bob Gibson striking out 17 Tigers in '68, and now Orel Hershiser.

Despite Jose Canseco's second-inning grand slam for Oakland in Game 1 of the World Series, L.A. did not have an ounce of quit, and

All-1980s Dodgers Team

Position	Name
Pitcher	Orel Hershiser
Pitcher	Bob Welch
Pitcher	Fernando Valenzuela
Pitcher	Jerry Reuss
Relief Pitcher	Jay Howell
Catcher	Mike Sciosca
First Baseman	Steve Garvey
Second Baseman	Steve Sax
Third Baseman	Ron Cey
Shortstop	Bill Russell
Outfielder	Kirk Gibson
Outfielder	Pedro Guerrero
Outfielder	Mike Marshall
Manager	Tommy Lasorda

trailed only 4–3 in the ninth against ace closer Dennis Eckersley. With two out and none on, Mike Davis somehow drew a walk against the control expert Eck. How Eckersley managed to throw four wide ones against Davis—a guy who had not been a threat since hitting a double to give this author's high school team its first loss of the season my senior year—remains, like much of that season, a mystery.

Kirk Gibson had a bum knee, his career was effectively already over, but he was called on to pinch hit. Why didn't Lasorda use him sooner, like when Davis was up there with two outs and it was now-or-never? For whatever reason, and that year the reasons just added up right, Tommy waited. Eckersley dominated Gibby up to a two-strike count, his moving, blazing fastball almost knocking the bat out of Kirk's hands. The ball Gibson hit out of the park to win it was almost in the dirt. The same hand of destiny that controlled Hershiser's 10-inning eclipse of Drysdale's record somehow lifted, golf swing–style, that baseball into the right-field pavilion.

The rest, of course, was quite predictable at that point. On Sunday night Hershiser threw a three-hit shutout. By this time, just getting a hit off the man almost seemed worthy of headlines the same size as, say, "Kennedy Murder Solved" or "Osama in Custody."

TRIVIA

How many consecutive years did the Dodgers have the National League Rookie of the Year?

Answers to the trivia questions are on pages 178–179

By the time Hershiser wrapped up a complete-game, four-hit victory to give Los Angeles a 4–1 Series victory and earn himself the fall classic's Most Valuable Player award, the Oakland fans were reduced to watching and admiring the guy.

Piazza

The Dodgers have stumbled badly since their 1988 world championship. The reason can be summed up in two words: News Corporation. Peter O'Malley claimed that federal estate taxes were so egregious that his heirs could not afford to inherit the team from him. Whether this is true or not, the fact is that when O'Malley sold the team to corporate interests, all the mystique of a fabled franchise was lost. It will take a true baseball magician to return them to glory, but he is out there...somewhere.

News Corporation is, in itself, a fine company, run by entertainment mogul Rupert Murdoch. Their holdings include Fox News, book publishers, movie studios, radio stations, and other parts of the conglomeration. But running a baseball team is different.

They put Bob Daly in charge. He was a movie big shot, which is like asking Tommy Lasorda to run Paramount. He'd probably have 'em remake *The Godfather,* only this time not portray Italian Americans as criminals. The results of Daly's tenure were just as disastrous from the baseball perspective. The most egregious error made by the Dodgers occurred in 1998 when Mike Piazza, the greatest offensive catcher in baseball history, was let go because the Dodgers, one of pro sports' richest organizations, anticipated his salary demands would be too great.

Piazza was bred to be a Dodger. His father, Vince, was born just a few blocks away from Lasorda in Norristown, Pennsylvania. They were distant cousins whose friendship lasted all their lives. Vincent became a millionaire used-car dealer. Vince's son, Mike, served as the Dodgers' ballboy when they played at Philadelphia.

Future Hall of Famer Mike Piazza was signed as a favor by Tom Lasorda, a friend of his father's, then matured into the best-hitting catcher of all time.

Vince built his son a batting cage and even arranged private lessons with Ted Williams, who was impressed.

"I guarantee you, this kid will hit the ball," Williams told Vince.

A prep first baseman, Piazza was not considered a prospect for reasons that seem odd looking back, but were centered on a lack of defensive skills. He could not run and his arm was considered suspect, but his hitting was never in doubt.

He went to the University of Miami, but he did not cut it there and enrolled in a junior college. Lasorda, as a favor to Vince, arranged for the Dodgers to draft him in the 62nd round, the 1,389th player picked in 1988. Drafting a player does not obligate the club to offer him a contract, and the Dodgers had no intention of doing so. Vince and Lasorda felt that his getting drafted would help him land

That in the early 1990s, the Dodgers had a team distinctively made up of "hometown heroes"? Among the players from the L.A. area were Eddie Murray, Darryl Strawberry, Brett Butler, Gary Carter, Chris Gwynn, Bob Ojeda, Eric Karros, Eric Davis, Jim Gott, Kevin Gross, and Tim Wallach. They contended but also struggled. Some of the players were over-the-hill, injured, or suffered off-the-field problems.

another Division I scholarship offer, but that did not happen. Out of desperation, Lasorda arranged a tryout. Piazza hit the ball well, and the club decided to try him as a catcher.

In the minor leagues, Piazza's work ethic paid off. He went to the club's baseball academy in the Dominican Republic to hone his catching skills, developing good qualities behind the plate. Everywhere he went Piazza hit well, and by 1993 he was a big-league prospect. Nobody could have predicted what happened next, though.

Piazza took the baseball world by storm with one of the greatest rookie years in the game's history, blasting 35 homers and batting .318. He made the All-Star team. His matinee-idol good looks made him an immediate star in L.A., his name linked with actresses and *Playboy* centerfolds.

Lasorda went crazy over the kid, talking him up constantly. He was a one-man public relations machine for his friend's son. It was an incredible story, even less likely than Fernando's.

The time was just right to rebuild the Dodgers. In 1994 the leagues split into East, West, and Central Divisions. The perennial National League champion Braves moved to the East, leaving it wide open for a team to assert themselves in the other divisions. But Dodger mistakes before and after the Murdoch acquisition had the effect of destroying the team instead of building them around Piazza. Two factors contributed to this. First, Ramon Martinez came down with arm problems and never realized his full potential, which was at Cooperstown level. Second, the Dodgers failed to recognize the potential of Ramon's younger brother, Pedro. He was traded to Montreal and went on to superstardom that actually *is* at Cooperstown level.

Piazza was a total star with no supporting cast until his ignominious trade to Florida, which eventually resulted in his becoming a New York Met. L.A. has usually been an also-ran in the years since, forced to play the role of the Washington Generals to Barry Bonds's Globetrotters (Bonds seemingly hit all his most momentous home runs versus the Dodgers).

There was one moment during Piazza's Dodger career in which L.A. got the better of San Francisco, however. Entering the last day of the 1993 season, San Francisco and Atlanta were tied for the National League West lead with 103 wins apiece. While the Braves won, Piazza cracked two home runs and the Dodgers crushed the Giants' hopes, 12–1, before a cheering, jeering crowd.

"They beat us in '91 and laughed at us," remembered infielder Lenny Harris. "Let them sit home during the fall classic and see how we felt."

As great as Piazza was, the team seemed snakebit during his time there. L.A. schoolboy hero Darryl Strawberry was brought on board, along with his childhood friend Eric Davis. Even though neither was old, aside from Strawberry's first year they did little to nothing for the Dodgers. In Strawberry's case, drugs took over his life, an addiction he battles to this day.

Raul Mondesi looked to be a five-tool player in the mold of Roberto Clemente, but he did not have what it took when all was said and done. Japanese import Hideo Nomo caused big excitement at first with his strong pitching performances, but when the league figured him out, he became barely above average.

TRIVIA

Who did the Dodgers get for Mike Piazza?

Answers to the trivia questions are on pages 178–179

Eric Karros came off the UCLA campus and was a consistent power hitter. He and Piazza shared a beach pad in the South Bay. Stories of their prowess with the ladies became legendary along the Strand. But Karros, despite good numbers, always seemed to get his hits when they meant little. He reminded nobody of Steve Garvey or Gil Hodges.

Another power-hitting Bruin, Todd Zeile, was the perfect Dodger. He wanted to break into the film business—not just as an actor but as a producer—and should have enjoyed a long, successful Tinseltown run, but he was lost after just a little more than one full season.

Chan Ho Park, a hard-throwing Korean, was another disappointment. His unlimited potential never got much past the "potential" part. The Dodgers of the mid-1990s made some playoff appearances, but never won playoff games. Eventually, they lost the Pacific Coast power struggle with the Giants and Padres, not to mention the Rockies, who had good teams built around their mile-high hitter's park.

In 1997 Piazza was on fire, batting .362 with 40 homers. Unfortunately, the BALCO steroid scandals of the 2000s revealed that many players were "juiced," and much of the worst abuse took place in the mid-1990s. Piazza was a workout fiend, to be sure, but he, along with all other offensive superstars of this incredible "hitter's era," must be looked back on now with some suspicion.

The Poet

Vin Scully has the longest consecutive service of any current major league broadcaster with a single team. He *is* the Dodgers, more so than Walter or Peter O'Malley; Sandy Koufax or Don Drysdale; or even Jackie Robinson.

"Scully has the most musical voice in baseball," wrote Gary Kaufman for Salon.com in 1999. "He doesn't have the clipped, old-time-radio cadence of most broadcasters who date back to the '50s and beyond. Although his timbre is thin, everything is smooth and rounded. The words slide into each other. He has flow. The melody rises and falls on the tide of the game. You can almost hum along to Vin Scully."

"At times I'll be listening to him and I'll think, Oh, I wish I could call upon that expression the way he does," Dick Enberg has said. "He paints the picture more beautifully than anyone who's ever called a baseball game."

Most sports announcers have grown up idolizing Scully. Some do a pretty fair imitation of him, the best being San Francisco and ESPN announcer Jon Miller's impersonations, particularly his self-deprecating Scully-riff on himself, "And then there's Jon Miller, the best broadcaster in baseball *in his price range!*"

Scully's L.A. connection has made him an oft-heard voice in movies and TV, highlighted by his role as himself in Kevin Costner's movie *For Love of the Game.*

Baseball is much more of a TV game than it used to be, and Scully has done as much television work as radio in recent years, but he was *made* for radio. He is one of the last broadcasters to work alone, without a "color man." On NBC's *Game of the Week*, his partner

TRIVIA

Who holds the Dodger record for home runs in a single season by a right-handed batter?

Answers to the trivia questions are on pages XXX–XXX

was Joe Garagiola. Scully told Garagiola he did not want Joe telling *him* about inside baseball.

"You tell the *fans* the 'inside baseball,'" he said. "But don't tell me."

The Hall of Famer Scully has done it all in L.A. and on a national level. He handled the *Game of the Week* broadcasts before ESPN and Fox Sports became the prevalent sports cable stations. His partner for one season was former New York Met superstar Tom Seaver. He has also handled the NFL and the PGA Tour.

But Scully stood above all of them in Mt. Rushmore style.

He has had radio partners, of course. Jerry Doggett was there to let him take bathroom breaks. Ross Porter was better than Doggett. But his partner's best traits have always been that they knew not to upstage Vinnie.

Scully is a native New Yorker.

The family was "not poverty-stricken, just poor," he said. "I was about eight years old and we had an old radio on four legs with crossed bars between the legs," he told his friend Danny Kaye in a TV tribute in 1982, "and I would come home to listen to a football game—there weren't other sports on—and I would get a pillow and I would crawl under the radio, so that the loudspeaker and the roar of the crowd would wash all over me, and I would just get goose bumps like you can't believe. And I knew that of all the things in this world that I wanted, I wanted to be that fella saying, whatever, home run, or touchdown. It just really got to me."

Scully played baseball on a partial scholarship at Fordham University, served in the navy, then went to work at a local radio station while stringing for *The New York Times*.

When Red Barber needed an announcer for a college football game as part of his "Saturday CBS Football Roundup," he called Scully at his parents' home.

"What kind of mother would I have?" Scully said. "Irish, red-headed, and excitable. She took the message, but she said it was from Red Skelton."

Scully's performance from Fenway Park impressed Barber. He offered him the job as number three man in the Dodgers' booth. He was 22 years old.

"We just needed somebody to sort of take an inning here and there and just do little things," Scully told Gary Kaufman.

"As I put it, carry our briefcases if necessary," said Barber, known as the Old Redhead, who was Scully's mentor. "Scully was a very apt young man. And he took right over. He made the most of his opportunity."

Scully picked up many of Barber's cadences. In particular, Barber's call of Cookie Lavagetto's game-winning double in Game 4 of the 1947 World Series ("Here comes the tying run, and heeeeere comes the *winning* run!") sounds almost exactly like Scully.

"Red never taught me how to broadcast, he never taught me baseball, or anything like that," Scully said in the 1982 video. "What

When it comes to the Dodgers, the last word always belongs to Vin Scully. A baseball poet, Scully is well regarded as the finest announcer the game has ever heard.

All-Time Greatest Baseball Announcers

1. Vin Scully (Dodgers)
2. Ernie Harwell
3. Red Barber (Dodgers)
4. Jack Buck
5. Lon Simmons
6. Curt Gowdy
7. Mel Allen
8. Bob Uecker
9. Bob Prince
10. Harry Caray

he did teach me was, among other things, an attitude—get there early and do your homework and bear down. Use the crowd."

Scully's "use of the crowd" technique was fairly new. Many older broadcasters of his early years had come up doing recreations from studios, where they had to conjure the action seemingly out of whole cloth. But he was never a fan of Hodges's maniacal call of the Thomson homer, preferring to let the story tell itself without histrionics.

When Koufax struck out Harvey Kuenn to complete his perfect game, Scully stayed quiet for 38 seconds while the crowd roared. When Henry Aaron broke Babe Ruth's career home-run record with his 715th in 1974, Scully said, "It's gone!" Then he took off his headset.

When the Brooklyn Dodgers won the 1955 World Series, his description was simply: "Ladies and gentlemen, the Brooklyn Dodgers are the champions of the world."

Barber became too expensive at $60,000 per year. O'Malley got rid of him. He moved over to the Yankees and Scully was the number one man for the Dodgers...at $18,000 a year. In 1958 the Dodgers moved to Los Angeles.

"My first feeling was of tremendous relief when [O'Malley] told me I was in his plans to go to Los Angeles," Scully told Bob Raissman of the *New York Daily News* in 1997. "But I was saddened because being a New Yorker, everything I had and loved in the world was back there."

Despite being a native of the Bronx, Scully's voice is not distinctively New York, perhaps because he honed his skills under the Southerner Barber. He was an immediate hit in L.A., and for reasons as mystical as any, has always been perfect for that city; the voice emanating from car radios, or transistors held to ears in the stands (a common Dodger Stadium practice in the early years).

Scully was married in 1958 and had three children, but his wife passed away in 1972. In 1959 he was able to broadcast L.A.'s first world championship. In 1965, on the last day of the season, with the Dodgers having clinched the pennant the night before, manager Walter Alston let Scully manage, over the radio, from the booth.

When Ron Fairly—who had done a little bit of drinking in celebration the night before—drew a walk, Scully described it as, "He didn't trot to first base. He didn't really walk to first base. He *sloshed* to first base."

Then, given the power to manage the game, he ordered the already slow Fairly to steal second.

"For those of you in the ballpark with transistor radios listening," Scully said, "watch Fairly's face when he looks over to third and gets the steal sign."

Fairly staired incredulously but took off. As if to torture him, a foul ball sent Ron back to first, and Scully sent him a second time. When the catcher dropped the ball, Fairly made it safely.

"All right, Walter," he said, "I got you this far. Now you're on your own."

Scully went through a personal crisis when his first wife passed away, and even took some time off from road trips, but married again. He has three more children from his second wife. That marriage seemed to be his saving grace, although fans listening to him never heard him complain or give less than his very best.

By the NUMBERS

5—The number of L.A. Dodgers to collect 200 hits in a season. Adrian Beltre accomplished the feat in 2004.

ANSWERS TO TRIVIA QUESTIONS

Page 5: Four. Pitcher "Iron Joe" McGinnity, first baseman Hughie "Ee-Yah" Jennings, outfielder Willie "Hit 'em Where They Ain't" Keeler, and manager Ned Hanlon.

Page 15: Rogers Hornsby said he was "the perfect free swinger," as natural and flawless as Babe Ruth.

Page 21: On June 15, 1938. Cincinnati's Johnny Vander Meer threw his second straight no-hitter versus the Dodgers, winning 6–0.

Page 28: "Fat Freddie" Fitzsimmons, who pitched a shutout until an injury forced him to leave a game eventually won by New York, 2–0.

Page 38: He was born in the Deep South—Cairo, Georgia—but moved with his family to Pasadena as a young child.

Page 40: Dick Littlefield and $30,000. The trade seemed to portend the last ties between the Dodgers and Brooklyn. Instead of becoming Willie Mays's teammate in New York and later in San Francisco, however, Robinson chose retirement, an executive position with the Chock Full o'Nuts candy company, and an exclusive article in *Look* magazine. The trade was rescinded.

Page 48: Berra bragged that the previous year in the minor leagues, when Berra was at Newark and Robinson played for Montreal, Robinson had not successfully stolen a base against him. Robinson stole second base in the first inning and after the game told reporters, "If I ran against Berra every day I'd steal 60 bases."

Page 53: While Clyde Sukeforth, a trusted advisor, is credited with signing Robinson, it was ex-St. Louis Browns' Hall of Famer George Sisler who provided a blunt, honest assessment of Robinson as a player and competitor. Sisler played for Rickey at the University of Michigan and with the Browns. He was "like a son" to him.

Page 57: "Luck is the residue of design."

Page 72: It was for "unpleasant incidents detrimental to baseball."

Page 79: Clyde Sukeforth, the scout who along with George Sisler was credited with the discovery and signing of Jackie Robinson, and a one-time Brooklyn manager, was fired for recommending Ralph Branca over Clem Labine because he told Dressen that Labine was bouncing his curve in the bullpen.

Page 87: Eighth (1,033,589).

Page 97: "They took the bat away from you. You're done, man."

Page 101: O'Malley planned the first ever pay-cable station called Skiatron. He hated "free TV" because fans could stay at home to see games instead of buying tickets. Political and technical difficulties prevented the creation of Skiatron. O'Malley only allowed KTTV/11 to televise road games after much consternation. For years before Prime Ticket, ESPN, Fox, and other cable channels, the Dodgers were one of the least televised teams, virtually never showing a home game and reducing road contests to the Giants and about one game per season with each National League opponent. Today, almost all road and home games are on TV in one way or another.

Page 106: Pee Wee Reese, who had just retired. But coach Charlie Dressen and Leo Durocher, in limbo at the time, were hot names. Alston was retained.

Page 112: He resided in a ranch-style house in Studio City, set up against a heavily landscaped hill west of Ventura Boulevard behind a high retaining wall at the end of a curving, narrow street that made it well out of the way. Koufax had a large collection of records with an emphasis on classical music. His interests were eclectic: music, fine dining, theatre, gardening, golf, and, according to David Plaut's *Chasing October*, "the company of attractive women."

Page 115: "How come he lost fives games this year?" Tony Kubek asked the rhetorical question "Do they [National League hitters] hit him any better in September after seeing him all season?" Mickey Mantle: "His fastball must sink or hop or something."

Page 120: "I bet you wish I was Jewish too."

Page 127: Knowing how few runs the Dodgers scored, he asked, "Did he win?"

Page 135: Under Buzzie Bavasi, L.A. had not made a significant midseason trade since acquiring Sal Maglie in 1956. With Billy Grabarkewitz not hitting, O'Malley okayed the trade of Ron Fairly and Paul Popovich to the expansion Montreal Expos for the "disloyal" Maury Wills and pinch-hitter extraordinaire Manny Mota.

Page 143: Frank Howard, Dick Nen, Phil Ortega, and Pete Richert were sent to the Washington Senators for $100,000 and shortstop John Kennedy and pitcher Claude

Osteen. When Tommy Davis suffered a season-ending injury early in 1965, the loss of Howard's power seemed insurmountable, but Osteen's clutch pitching made the trade pay off. In '74 Osteen was traded to Houston for Jimmy Wynn, who starred for L.A.

Page 147: Al Downing briefly reached the potential in L.A. (20 wins in 1971) he had been expected to reach with the Yankees, but his career never really matched ultimate expectations. His fastball to Aaron looks on ESPN Classic replays to be a straight-as-an-arrow batting practice "fast" ball.

Page 153: The "Big Dodger in the Sky."

Page 157: Jackie Robinson's 42, Roy Campanella's 39, and Sandy Koufax's 32, in a 1972 Dodger Stadium ceremony. In 1997 Major League Baseball retired Robinson's number 42 from all future big-league teams.

Page 161: "You can plant 2,000 rows of corn with the fertilizer he spreads around."

Page 167: Four. Rick Sutcliffe (1979), Steve Howe (1980), Fernando Valenzuela (1981), and Steve Sax (1982). They had the Rookie of the Year five straight years in the 1990s: Eric Karros (1992), Mike Piazza (1993), Raul Mondesi (1994), Hideo Nomo (1995), and Todd Hollandsworth (1996).

Page 171: It was ultimately a complicated trade involving three teams, but the main part of the deal involved Gary Sheffield coming over from the then-defending 1997 world champion Florida Marlins for Piazza in May 1998. Sheffield averaged 36 homers with a .316 batting average until he was traded to Atlanta in 2002.

Page 174: Adrian Beltre, with 48 in 2004.

Dodgers All-Time Roster (through 2006 season)

A

Don Aase (P)	1990
Bert Abbey (P)	1895–96
Cal Abrams (OF)	1949–52
Tony Abreu (SS)	2006
Terry Adams (P)	2000–01
Morrie Aderholt (OF)	1944–45
Hank Aguirre (P)	1968
Eddie Ainsmith (C)	1923
Kurt Ainsworth (P)	2006
Raleigh Aitchison (P)	1911–15
Ed Albosta (P)	1941
Luis Alcaraz (2B)	1967–68
Doyle Alexander (P)	1971
Mark Alexander (P)	2006
Dick Allen (1B)	1971
Frank Allen (P)	1912–14
Horace Allen (OF)	1919
Johnny Allen (P)	1941, 1942–43
Luke Allen (OF)	2002
Mel Almada (OF)	1939
Sandy Alomar (C)	2006
Whitey Alperman (2B)	1906–09
Carlos Alvarez (P)	2006
Nick Alvarez (1B)	2006
Orlando Alvarez (OF)	1973–75
Victor Alvarez (P)	2002
Wilson Alvarez (P)	2003–05
Ed Amelung (OF)	1984–86

Sandy Amoros (OF)	1952–57, 1959, 1960
Dave Anderson (SS)	1983–89, 1992
Ferrell Anderson (C)	1946
John Anderson (OF)	1894–98, 1899
Stan Andrews (C)	1944–45
Pat Ankenman (2B)	1943–44
Eric Anthony (OF)	1997
Bill Antonello (OF)	1953
Ed Appleton (P)	1915–16
Jimmy Archer (C)	1918
Jamie Arnold (P)	1999–2000
Andy Ashby (P)	2001–03
Billy Ashley (OF)	1992–97
Bob Aspromonte (3B)	1956, 1960–61
Pedro Astacio (P)	1992–97
Rick Auerbach (SS)	1974–76
Bruce Aven (OF)	2000–01
Willy Aybar (3B)	2005–06

B

Charlie Babb (SS)	1904–05
Johnny Babich (P)	1934–35
Danys Baez (P)	2006
Bob Bailey (3B)	1967–68
Gene Bailey (OF)	1923–24
Sweetbreads Bailey (P)	1921
Bob Bailor (OF)	1984–85
Doug Baird (3B)	1919, 1920
Dusty Baker (OF)	1976–83

Tom Baker (P)	1935–37	Ike Benners (OF)	1884
Paul Bako (C)	2005	Todd Benzinger (1B)	1992
James Baldwin (P)	2001	Moe Berg (C)	1923
Lady Baldwin (P)	1890	Bill Bergen (C)	1904–11
Win Ballou (P)	1929	Ray Berres (C)	1934–36
Dave Bancroft (SS)	1928–29	Geronimo Berroa (DH)	2000
Dan Bankhead (P)	1947–51	Don Bessent (P)	1955–57, 1958
Willie Banks (P)	1995	Wilson Betemit (3B)	2006
Jack Banta (P)	1947–50	Dante Bichette (OF)	2002
Turner Barber (OF)	1923	Nick Bierbrodt (P)	2006
Jim Barbieri (OF)	1966	Steve Bilko (1B)	1958
Cy Barger (P)	1910–12	Jack Billingham (P)	1968
Red Barkley (2B)	1943	Chad Billingsley (P)	2006
Brian Barnes (P)	1994	Ralph Birkofer (P)	1937
Jesse Barnes (P)	1926–27	Babe Birrer (P)	1958
Larry Barnes (1B)	2003	Del Bissonette (1B)	1928–33
Rex Barney (P)	1943–50	Joe Black (P)	1952–55
Bob Barr (P)	1935	Henry Blanco (C)	1997
Bob Barrett (3B)	1925, 1927	Clarence Blethen (P)	1929
Manuel Barrios (P)	1998	Mike Blowers (3B)	1996
Boyd Bartley (SS)	1943	Lu Blue (1B)	1933
Al Bashang (OF)	1918	Hiram Bocachica (OF)	2000–02
Eddie Basinski (SS)	1944–45	Doug Bochtler (P)	1999
Emil Batch (3B)	1904–07	George Boehler (P)	1926
Jim Baxes (2B)	1959	Tim Bogar (SS)	2001
Bill Bean (OF)	1989	Brian Bohanon (P)	1998
Boom–Boom Beck (P)	1933–34	Sam Bohne (2B)	1926
Erve Beck (2B)	1899	Jack Bolling (1B)	1944
Joe Beckwith (P)	1979–83, 1986	Ricky Bones (P)	2002
Hank Behrman (P)	1946–47, 1948	Bobby Bonilla (3B)	1998
Joe Beimel (P)	2006	Frank Bonner (2B)	1896
Kevin Beirne (P)	2001–02	Ike Boone (OF)	1930–32
Mark Belanger (SS)	1982	Pedro Borbon (P)	1998–99
Wayne Belardi (1B)	1950–54	Frenchy Bordagaray (OF)	1935–36, 1942–45
Tim Belcher (P)	1987–91	Pat Borders (C)	2006
Frank Bell (C)	1885	Bob Borkowski (OF)	1955
George Bell (P)	1907–11	Rafael Bournigal (SS)	1992–94
Edwin Bellorin (C)	2006	Ken Boyer (3B)	1968–69
Adrian Beltre (3B)	1998–2004	Buzz Boyle (OF)	1933–35
Ray Benge (P)	1933–35	Gibby Brack (OF)	1937–38

Mark Bradley (OF)	1981–82	Ralph Bryant (OF)	1985–87
Milton Bradley (OF)	2004–05	Jim Bucher (3B)	1934–37
Joe Bradshaw (P)	1929	Bill Buckner (1B)	1969–76
Bobby Bragan (SS)	1943–48	Cy Buker (P)	1945
Ralph Branca (P)	1944–53, 1956	Jim Bullinger (P)	2000
Ed Brandt (P)	1936	Jim Bunning (P)	1969
Jeff Branson (3B)	2000–01	Al Burch (OF)	1907, 1908–11
Craig Brazell (1B)	2006	Ernie Burch (OF)	1886–87
Yhency Brazoban (P)	2004–06	Jack Burdock (2B)	1888, 1891
Sid Bream (1B)	1983–85	Sandy Burk (P)	1910–12
Marv Breeding (2B)	1963	Glenn Burke (OF)	1976–78
Tom Brennan (P)	1985	Jeromy Burnitz (OF)	2003
William Brennan (P)	1988	Oyster Burns (OF)	1888–89, 1890–95
Rube Bressler (OF)	1928–31	Buster Burrell (C)	1895–97
Ken Brett (P)	1979	Larry Burright (2B)	1962
Jim Brewer (P)	1964–75	Mike Busch (3B)	1995–96
Tony Brewer (OF)	1984	Doc Bushong (C)	1888–89, 1890
Rocky Bridges (SS)	1951–52	Max Butcher (P)	1936–38
Greg Brock (1B)	1982–86	Brett Butler (OF)	1991–95, 1996–97
Matt Broderick (2B)	1903	John Butler (C)	1906–07
Troy Brohawn (P)	2003	Johnny Butler (SS)	1926–27
Hubie Brooks (OF)	1990		
Jerry Brooks (OF)	1993	**C**	
Dan Brouthers (1B)	1892–93	Enos Cabell (3B)	1985–86
Eddie Brown (OF)	1924–25	Jolbert Cabrera (OF)	2002–03
Elmer Brown (P)	1913–15	Leon Cadore (P)	1915–23
John Brown (P)	1897	Bruce Caldwell (OF)	1932
Kevin Brown (P)	1999–2003	Leo Callahan (OF)	1913
Lindsay Brown (SS)	1937	Dick Calmus (P)	1963
Lloyd Brown (P)	1925	Dolph Camilli (1B)	1938–43
Mace Brown (P)	1941	Doug Camilli (C)	1960–64
Tommy Brown (SS)	1944–51	Roy Campanella (C)	1948–57
George Browne (OF)	1911	Al Campanis (2B)	1943
Pete Browning (OF)	1894	Jim Campanis (C)	1966–68
Jonathan Broxton (P)	2005–06	Gilly Campbell (C)	1938
Bruce Brubaker (P)	1967	Jim Canavan (OF)	1897
Cole Bruce (SS)	2006	John Candelaria (P)	1991–92
Jacob Brumfield (OF)	1999	Tom Candiotti (P)	1992–97
Will Brunson (P)	1998	Chris Cannizzaro (C)	1972–73
Jim Bruske (P)	1995–96, 1998	Guy Cantrell (P)	1925–27

Ben Cantwell (P)	1937
Andy Carey (3B)	1962
Max Carey (OF)	1926, 1927–29
Tex Carleton (P)	1940
Buddy Carlyle (P)	2005
Giovanni Carrara (P)	2001–06
Ownie Carroll (P)	1933–34
Kid Carsey (P)	1901
Gary Carter (C)	1991
Lance Carter (P)	2006
Bob Caruthers (OF)	1888–89, 1890–91
Hugh Casey (P)	1939–48
Doc Casey (3B)	1899, 1900, 1906–07
John Cassidy (OF)	1884–85
Pete Cassidy (1B)	1899
Bobby Castillo (P)	1977–81, 1985
Juan Castro (SS)	1995–99
Tom Catterson (OF)	1908–09
Cesar Cedeno (OF)	1986
Roger Cedeno (OF)	1995–98
Ron Cey (3B)	1971–82
Ed Chandler (P)	1947
Ben Chapman (OF)	1944–45
Glenn Chapman (OF)	1934
Robinson Checo (P)	1999–2000
Chin-Feng Chen (LF)	2002, 2004–05
Larry Cheney (P)	1915, 1916–19
Paul Chervinko (C)	1937–38
Bob Chipman (P)	1941–44
Hee-Seop Choi (1B)	2004–06
McKay Christensen (OF)	2001
Mike Christopher (P)	1991
Chuck Churn (P)	1959
Gino Cimoli (OF)	1956–57, 1958
George Cisar (OF)	1937
Moose Clabaugh (OF)	1926
Bud Clancy (1B)	1932
Bob Clark (C)	1886–89, 1890
Dave Clark (OF)	1996
Watty Clark (P)	1927–33, 1934, 1935–37

Wally Clement (OF)	1909
Brad Clontz (P)	1998
Alta Cohen (OF)	1931–32
Rocky Colavito (OF)	1968
Bill Collins (OF)	1913
Hub Collins (2B)	1888, 1889, 1890–92
Jackie Collum (P)	1957, 1958
Steve Colyer (P)	2003
Chuck Connors (1B)	1949
Jim Conway (P)	1884
Dennis Cook (P)	1990–91
Brent Cookson (OF)	1999
Jack Coombs (P)	1915–18
Ron Coomer (1B)	2003
Johnny Cooney (OF)	1935–37, 1943–44
Alex Cora (SS)	1998–2004
Claude Corbitt (SS)	1945
Jack Corcoran (C)	1884
Tommy Corcoran (SS)	1892–96
Bryan Corey (P)	2002
Chuck Corgan (SS)	1925–27
Pop Corkhill (OF)	1888–89, 1890
Pete Coscarart (2B)	1938–41
Bob Coulson (OF)	1910–11
Craig Counsell (2B)	1999
Wes Covington (OF)	1966
Billy Cox (3B)	1948–54
Dick Cox (OF)	1925–26
George Crable (P)	1910
Roger Craig (P)	1955–61
Ed Crane (P)	1893
Sam Crane (SS)	1922
Willie Crawford (OF)	1964–75
Tim Crews (P)	1987–92
Claude Crocker (P)	1944–45
Tripp Cromer (SS)	1996–99
Jack Cronin (P)	1895, 1904
Bubba Crosby (OF)	2003
Lave Cross (3B)	1900
Bill Crouch (P)	1939

Don Crow (C)	1982	Willie Davis (OF)	1960–73
Henry Cruz (OF)	1975–76	Pea Ridge Day (P)	1931
Jose Cruz (OF)	2005–06	Lindsay Deal (OF)	1939
Tony Cuccinello (2B)	1932–35	Tommy Dean (SS)	1967
Roy Cullenbine (OF)	1940	Hank DeBerry (C)	1922–30
Nick Cullop (OF)	1929	Art Decatur (P)	1922–25
George Culver (P)	1973	Artie Dede (C)	1916
John Cummings (P)	1995–96	Rod Dedeaux (SS)	1935
Bert Cunningham (P)	1887	Pat Deisel (C)	1902
Chad Curtis (OF)	1996	Ivan DeJesus (SS)	1974–76
Cliff Curtis (P)	1912–13	Ivan DeJesus (SS)	2006
George Cutshaw (2B)	1912–17	Wheezer Dell (P)	1915–17
Kiki Cuyler (OF)	1938	Bert Delmas (2B)	1933
		Don Demeter (OF)	1956, 1958–61
D		Gene Demontreville (2B)	1900
Omar Daal (P)	1993–95, 2002	Rick Dempsey (C)	1988–90
Bill Dahlen (SS)	1899–1903, 1910–11	Travis Denker (2B)	2006
Babe Dahlgren (1B)	1942	Eddie Dent (P)	1909–12
Con Daily (C)	1891–95	Delino DeShields (2B)	1993–96
Jud Daley (OF)	1911–12	John Desilva (P)	1993
Jack Dalton (OF)	1910–14	Rube Dessau (P)	1910
Tom Daly (2B)	1890–1901	Elmer Dessens (P)	2004–06
Jake Daniel (1B)	1937	Mike Devereaux (OF)	1987–88, 1998
Kal Daniels (OF)	1989–92	Blake Dewitt (2B)	2006
Fats Dantonio (C)	1944–45	Carlos Diaz (P)	1984–86
Cliff Dapper (C)	1942	Jose Diaz (P)	2005–06
Bob Darnell (P)	1954–56	Leo Dickerman (P)	1923–24
Bobby Darwin (OF)	1969–71	Dick Dietz (C)	1972
Dan Daub (P)	1893–97	Pop Dillon (1B)	1904
Jake Daubert (1B)	1910–18	Glenn Dishman (P)	2002
Vic Davalillo (OF)	1977–80	Bill Doak (P)	1924, 1927–28
Bill Davidson (OF)	1910–11	John Dobbs (OF)	1903–05
Butch Davis (OF)	1991	George Dockins (P)	1947
Curt Davis (P)	1940, 1941–46	Cozy Dolan (OF)	1901–02
Eric Davis (OF)	1992–93	Chris Donnels (3B)	2000–01
Jumbo Davis (3B)	1889	Bill Donovan (P)	1899–1902
Lefty Davis (OF)	1901	Patsy Donovan (OF)	1890, 1906–07
Mike Davis (OF)	1988–89	Mickey Doolan (SS)	1918
Ron Davis (P)	1987	Jerry Dorgan (OF)	1884
Tommy Davis (OF)	1959–66	Jack Doscher (P)	1903–06

John Douglas (1B)	1945		Kid Elberfeld (SS)	1914
Phil Douglas (P)	1915		Jumbo Elliott (P)	1925–30
Snooks Dowd (2B)	1926		Rowdy Elliott (C)	1920
Red Downey (OF)	1909		Robert Ellis (P)	2002
Al Downing (P)	1971–77		Kevin Elster (SS)	2000
Red Downs (2B)	1912		Don Elston (P)	1957
Carl Doyle (P)	1939–40		Bones Ely (SS)	1891
Jack Doyle (1B)	1903–04		Juan Encarnacion (OF)	2004
Solly Drake (OF)	1959		Gil English (3B)	1944
Tom Drake (P)	1941		Woody English (SS)	1937–38
Darren Dreifort (P)	1994–2001, 2003–04		Johnny Enzmann (P)	1914
J.D. Drew (OF)	2005–06		Al Epperly (P)	1950
Don Drysdale (P)	1956–69		Scott Erickson (P)	2005
Clise Dudley (P)	1929–30		Carl Erskine (P)	1948–59
John Duffie (P)	1967		Tex Erwin (C)	1910–14
Jeff Duncan (OF)	2006		Cecil Espy (OF)	1983
Mariano Duncan (2B)	1985–87, 1989		Chuck Essegian (OF)	1959–60
Cory Dunlap (DH)	2006		Dude Esterbrook (3B)	1891
Jack Dunn (3B)	1897–1900		Andre Ethier (OF)	2006
Joe Dunn (C)	1908–09		Red Evans (P)	1939
Bull Durham (P)	1904		Roy Evans (P)	1902–03
Rich Durning (P)	1917–18			
Leo Durocher (SS)	1938–45		**F**	
Red Durrett (OF)			Bunny Fabrique (SS)	1916–17
			Jim Fairey (OF)	1968, 1973
E			Ron Fairly (1B)	1958–69
Billy Earle (C)	1894		Brian Falkenborg (P)	2004
George Earnshaw (P)	1935–36		George Fallon (2B)	1937
Mal Eason (P)	1905–06		Alex Farmer (C)	1908
Eddie Eayrs (OF)	1921		Duke Farrell (C)	1899, 1900–02
Ox Eckhardt (OF)	1936		Turk Farrell (P)	1961
Bruce Edwards (C)	1946–51		John Farrow (C)	1884
Hank Edwards (OF)	1951		Jim Faulkner (P)	1930
Mike Edwards (3B)	2005		Gus Felix (OF)	1926–27
Dick Egan (P)	1967		Alex Ferguson (P)	1929
Dick Egan (2B)	1914–15		Joe Ferguson (C)	1970–76, 1978–81
Rube Ehrhardt (P)	1924–28		Chico Fernandez (SS)	1956
Joey Eischen (P)	1995–96		Sid Fernandez (P)	1983
Jim Eisenreich (OF)	1998		Al Ferrara (OF)	1963–68
Harry Eisenstat (P)	1935–37		Wes Ferrell (P)	1940

Lou Fette (P)	1940
Mike Fetters (P)	2000–01
Chick Fewster (2B)	1926–27
Jack Fimple (C)	1983–86
Pembroke Finlayson (P)	1908–09
Steve Finley (OF)	2004
Neal Finn (2B)	1930–32
Jeff Fischer (P)	1989
William Fischer (C)	1913–14
Bob Fisher (SS)	1912–13
Chauncey Fisher (P)	1897
Freddie Fitzsimmons (P)	1937–43
Tom Fitzsimmons (3B)	1919
Darrin Fletcher (C)	1987–90
Sam Fletcher (P)	1909
Tim Flood (2B)	1902–03
Jose Flores (2B)	2004
Jake Flowers (2B)	1927–31, 1933
Wes Flowers (P)	1940–44
Chad Fonville (2B)	1995–97
Hod Ford (SS)	1925
Terry Forster (P)	1978–82
Alan Foster (P)	1967–70
Jack Fournier (1B)	1923–26
Dave Foutz (1B)	1888–89, 1890–96
Art Fowler (P)	1959
Fred Frankhouse (P)	1936–38
Jack Franklin (P)	1944
Herman Franks (C)	1940–41
Johnny Frederick (OF)	1929–34
Howard Freigau (3B)	1928
Larry French (P)	1941–42
Ray French (SS)	1923
Lonny Frey (2B)	1933–36
Pepe Frias (SS)	1980–81
Charlie Fuchs (P)	1944
Nig Fuller (C)	1902
Rafael Furcal (SS)	2005–06
Carl Furillo (OF)	1946–60

G

Len Gabrielson (OF)	1967–70
John Gaddy (P)	1938
Eric Gagne (P)	1999–2006
Greg Gagne (SS)	1996–97
Augie Galan (OF)	1941–46
Joe Gallagher (OF)	1940
Phil Gallivan (P)	1931
Balvino Galvez (P)	1986
Karim Garcia (OF)	1995–97
Sergio Garcia (2B)	2006
Nomar Garciaparra (SS)	2006
Mike Garman (P)	1977–78
Phil Garner (2B)	1987
Steve Garvey (1B)	1969–82
Ned Garvin (P)	1902–04
Welcome Gaston (P)	1898–99
Hank Gastright (P)	1894
Frank Gatins (3B)	1901
Sid Gautreaux (C)	1936–37
Billy Geer (SS)	1884
Jim Gentile (1B)	1957–58
Greek George (C)	1938
Ben Geraghty (SS)	1936
Doc Gessler (OF)	1903–06
Gus Getz (3B)	1914–16
Bob Giallombardo (P)	1958
Kirk Gibson (OF)	1988–90
Charlie Gilbert (OF)	1940
Pete Gilbert (3B)	1894
Shawn Gilbert (OF)	2000
Wally Gilbert (3B)	1928–31
Carden Gillenwater (OF)	1943
Jim Gilliam (2B)	1953–66
Al Gionfriddo (OF)	1947
Tony Giuliani (C)	1940–41
Al Glossop (2B)	1943
John Gochnauer (SS)	1901
Jim Golden (P)	1960–61
Dave Goltz (P)	1980–82

Jose Gonzalez (OF)	1985–91	Joel Guzman (LF)	2006
Luis E. Gonzalez (P)	2006	Chris Gwynn (OF)	1987–91, 1994–95
Johnny Gooch (C)	1928–29		
Ed Goodson (1B)	1976–77	**H**	
Tom Goodwin (OF)	1991–93, 2000–01	Bert Haas (1B)	1937–38
Ray Gordinier (P)	1921–22	George Haddock (P)	1892–93
Rick Gorecki (P)	1997	Chip Hale (DH)	1997
Jim Gott (P)	1990–94	John Hale (OF)	1974–77
Billy Grabarkewitz (3B)	1969–72	Bill Hall (P)	1913
Jason Grabowski (OF)	2004–05	Bob Hall (OF)	1905
Jack Graham (1B)	1946	Darren Hall (P)	1996–98
Jeff Granger (P)	2000	John Hall (P)	1948
Mudcat Grant (P)	1968	Toby Hall (C)	2006
Dick Gray (3B)	1958–59	Tom Haller (C)	1968–71
Harvey Green (P)	1935	Bill Hallman (2B)	1898
Shawn Green (OF)	2000–04	Jeff Hamilton (3B)	1986–91
Nelson Greene (P)	1924–25	Luke Hamlin (P)	1937–41
Kent Greenfield (P)	1929	Tim Hamulack (P)	2006
Bill Greenwood (2B)	1884	Gerry Hannahs (P)	1978–79
Ed Greer (OF)	1887	Pat Hannifan (OF)	1897
Hal Gregg (P)	1943–47	Greg Hansell (P)	1995
Alfredo Griffin (SS)	1988–91	Dave Hansen (3B)	1990–96, 1999–2002
Mike Griffin (OF)	1891–98	F.C. Hansford (P)	1898
Bert Griffith (OF)	1922–23	Charlie Hargreaves (C)	1923–28
Derrell Griffith (OF)	1963–66	Mike Harkey (P)	1997
Tommy Griffith (OF)	1919–25	John Harkins (P)	1885–87
John Grim (C)	1895–99	Tim Harkness (1B)	1961–62
Burleigh Grimes (P)	1918–26	George Harper (P)	1896
Dan Griner (P)	1918	Harry Harper (P)	1923
Lee Grissom (P)	1940–41	Bill Harris (P)	1957, 1959
Marquis Grissom (OF)	2001–02	Joe Harris (1B)	1928
Kevin Gross (P)	1991–94	Lenny Harris (3B)	1989–93
Kip Gross (P)	1992–93	Pep Harris (P)	2002
Jerry Grote (C)	1977–78, 1981	Bill Hart (P)	1892
Mark Grudzielanek (2B)	1998–2002	Bill Hart (3B)	1943–45
Pedro Guerrero (1B)	1978–88	Chris Hartje (C)	1939
Wilton Guerrero (2B)	1996–98	Mike Hartley (P)	1989–91
Brad Gulden (C)	1978	Buddy Hassett (1B)	1936–38
Ad Gumbert (P)	1895–96	Mickey Hatcher (OF)	1979–80, 1987–90
Mark Guthrie (P)	1995–98	Gil Hatfield (SS)	1893

Ray Hathaway (P)	1945	Bob Higgins (C)	1911–12
Joe Hatten (P)	1946–51	Andy High (3B)	1922–25
Chris Haughey (P)	1943	George Hildebrand (OF)	1902
Phil Haugstad (P)	1947–51	Bill Hill (P)	1899
Brad Havens (P)	1987–88	Koyie Hill (C)	2003
Jackie Hayes (C)	1884–85	Shawn Hillegas (P)	1987–88
Ray Hayworth (C)	1938–39, 1944–45	Hunkey Hines (OF)	1895
Ed Head (P)	1940–46	Mike Hines (C)	1885
Hughie Hearne (C)	1901–03	Don Hoak (3B)	1954–55
Mike Hechinger (C)	1913	Oris Hockett (OF)	1938–39
Danny Heep (OF)	1987–88	Gil Hodges (1B)	1943–61
Jake Hehl (P)	1918	Glenn Hoffman (SS)	1987
Fred Heimach (P)	1930–33	Jamie Hoffmann (CF)	2006
Harry Heitmann (P)	1918	Bert Hogg (3B)	1934
George Hemming (P)	1891	Bill Holbert (C)	1888
Hardie Henderson (P)	1886–87	Todd Hollandsworth (OF)	1995–2000
Rickey Henderson (OF)	2003	Al Hollingsworth (P)	1939
Harvey Hendrick (1B)	1927–31	Bonnie Hollingsworth (P)	1924
Mark Hendrickson (P)	2006	Damon Hollins (OF)	1998
Lafayette Henion (P)	1919	Darren Holmes (P)	1990
Weldon Henley (P)	1907	Jim Holmes (P)	1908
Butch Henline (C)	1927–29	Tommy Holmes (OF)	1952
Dutch Henry (P)	1923–24	Brian Holton (P)	1985–88
Roy Henshaw (P)	1937	Rick Honeycutt (P)	1983–87
Matt Herges (P)	1999–2001	Wally Hood (OF)	1920–22
Babe Herman (OF)	1926–31, 1945	Casey Hoorelbeke (P)	2006
Billy Herman (2B)	1941–46	Burt Hooton (P)	1975–84
Chad Hermansen (OF)	2003	Gail Hopkins (1B)	1974
Gene Hermanski (OF)	1943–51	Johnny Hopp (OF)	1949
Carlos Hernandez (C)	1990–96	Lefty Hopper (P)	1898
Enzo Hernandez (SS)	1978	Elmer Horton (P)	1898
Jose Hernandez (SS)	2004	Ricky Horton (P)	1988–89
Art Herring (P)	1934, 1944–46	Pete Hotaling (OF)	1885
Marty Herrmann (P)	1918	Charlie Hough (P)	1970–80
Orel Hershiser (P)	1983–94, 2000	D.J. Houlton (P)	2005–06
Greg Heydeman (P)	1973	Charlie Householder (1B)	1884
Phil Hiatt (3B)	2001	Ed Householder (OF)	1903
Jim Hickman (OF)	1916–19	Tyler Houston (3B)	2002
Jim Hickman (OF)	1967	Frank Howard (OF)	1958–64
Kirby Higbe (P)	1941–47	Thomas Howard (OF)	1998

Steve Howe (P)	1980–85	Randy Jackson (3B)	1956–58
Dixie Howell (C)	1953–56	Merwin Jacobson (OF)	1926–27
Harry Howell (P)	1898, 1900	Cleo James (OF)	1968
Jay Howell (P)	1988–92	Hal Janvrin (SS)	1921–22
Ken Howell (P)	1984–88	Roy Jarvis (C)	1944
Waite Hoyt (P)	1932, 1937–38	Stan Javier (OF)	1990–92
Chin Lung Hu (SS)	2006	George Jeffcoat (P)	1936–39
Trenidad Hubbard (OF)	1998–99	Jack Jenkins (P)	1969
Bill Hubbell (P)	1925	Hughie Jennings (SS)	1899–1900, 1903
Johnny Hudson (2B)	1936–40	Tommy John (P)	1972–78
Rex Hudson (P)	1974	Brian Johnson (C)	2000–01
Mike Huff (OF)	1989	Charles Johnson (C)	1998
Ed Hug (C)	1903	Lou Johnson (OF)	1965–67
Jay Hughes (P)	1899–1902	Fred Johnston (2B)	1924
Jim Hughes (P)	1952–56	Jimmy Johnston (3B)	1916–25
Mickey Hughes (P)	1888–89, 1890	Jay Johnstone (OF)	1980–82, 1985
Eric Hull (P)	2006	Art Jones (P)	1932
John Hummel (2B)	1905–15	Binky Jones (SS)	1924
Al Humphrey (OF)	1911	Charlie Jones (2B)	1884
Todd Hundley (C)	1999–2000, 2003	Fielder Jones (OF)	1896–1900
Bernie Hungling (C)	1922–23	Oscar Jones (P)	1903–05
Ron Hunt (2B)	1967	Brian Jordan (OF)	2002–03
George Hunter (OF)	1909–10	Dutch Jordan (2B)	1903–04
Willard Hunter (P)	1962	Jimmy Jordan (2B)	1933–36
Jerry Hurley (C)	1907	Ricardo Jordan (P)	1998–99
Joe Hutcheson (OF)	1933	Tim Jordan (1B)	1906–10
Ira Hutchinson (P)	1939	Spider Jorgensen (3B)	1947–50
Roy Hutson (OF)	1925	Von Joshua (OF)	1969–74, 1979
Tom Hutton (1B)	1966–69	Bill Joyce (3B)	1892
		William Juarez (P)	2006
I		Mike Judd (P)	1997–2001
Garey Ingram (2B)	1994–97	Joe Judge (1B)	1933
Bert Inks (P)	1891–92		
Charlie Irwin (3B)	1901–02	**K**	
Kaz Ishii (P)	2002–04	Alex Kampouris (2B)	1941–43
Cesar Izturis (SS)	2002–06	Eric Karros (1B)	1991–2002
		John Karst (3B)	1915
J		Willie Keeler (OF)	1893, 1899–1902
Fred Jacklitsch (C)	1903–04	Chet Kehn (P)	1942
Edwin Jackson (P)	2003–05	Mike Kekich (P)	1965–68

John Kelleher (3B)	1916	Ernie Koy (OF)	1938–40
Frank Kellert (1B)	1955	Ben Kozlowski (P)	2006
Joe Kelley (OF)	1899–1901	Chuck Kress (1B)	1954
Ryan Kellner (C)	2003–04	Chad Kreuter (C)	2000–02
George Kelly (1B)	1932	Bill Krieg (C)	1885
Roberto Kelly (OF)	1995	Bill Krueger (P)	1987–88
Matt Kemp (OF)	2006	Ernie Krueger (C)	1917–21
Bob Kennedy (OF)	1957	Abe Kruger (P)	1908
Brickyard Kennedy (P)	1892–1901	Jeff Kubenka (P)	1998–99
Ed Kennedy (OF)	1886	Hong-Chih Kuo (P)	2005–06
John Kennedy (3B)	1965–66	Jul Kustus (OF)	1909
Jeff Kent (2B)	2005–06		
Maury Kent (P)	1912–13	**L**	
Masao Kida (P)	2003–04	Clem Labine (P)	1950–60
Pete Kilduff (2B)	1919–21	Candy Lachance (1B)	1893–98
Newt Kimball (P)	1940–43	Lee Lacy (OF)	1972–78
Sam Kimber (P)	1884	Lerrin Lagrow (P)	1979
Clyde King (P)	1944–52	Frank Lamanske (P)	1935
Mike Kinkade (OF)	2002–03	Bill Lamar (OF)	1920–21
Tom Kinslow (C)	1891–94	Wayne Lamaster (P)	1938
Fred Kipp (P)	1957–59	Ray Lamb (P)	1969–70
Wayne Kirby (OF)	1996–97	Rafael Landestoy (2B)	1977, 1983–84
Enos Kirkpatrick (3B)	1912–13	Ken Landreaux (OF)	1981–87
Frank Kitson (P)	1900–02	Joe Landrum (P)	1950–52
Johnny Klippstein (P)	1958–59	Tito Landrum (OF)	1987
Joe Klugmann (2B)	1924	Eric Langill (C)	2003–06
Elmer Klump (P) (C)	1937	Frank Lankford (P)	1998
Elmer Knetzer (P)	1909–12	Norm Larker (1B)	1958–61
Hub Knolls (P)	1906	Andy LaRoche (3B)	2006
Eric Knott (P)	2003–04	Lyn Lary (SS)	1939
Jimmy Knowles (3B)	1884	Tom Lasorda (P)	1954–55
Barney Koch (2B)	1944	Tacks Latimer (C)	1902
Len Koenecke (OF)	1934–35	Cookie Lavagetto (3B)	1937–47
Paul Konerko (1B)	1994–98	Rudy Law (OF)	1978–80
Ed Konetchy (1B)	1919–21	Tony Lazzeri (2B)	1939
Jim Korwan (P)	1894	Bill Leard (2B)	1917
Andy Kosco (OF)	1969–70	Tim Leary (P)	1987–89
Sandy Koufax (P)	1955–66	Ricky Ledee (OF)	2005–06
Joe Koukalik (P)	1904	Aaron Ledesma (SS)	2000
Lou Koupal (P)	1928–29	Bob Lee (P)	1967

Hal Lee (OF)	1930	Eric Ludwick (P)	2002
Leron Lee (OF)	1975–76	Julio Lugo (SS)	2006
Jim Lefebvre (2B)	1965–72	Matt Luke (OF)	1998–99
Ken Lehman (P)	1952–57	Harry Lumley (OF)	1904–10
Larry Lejeune (OF)	1911	Don Lund (OF)	1945–48
Don LeJohn (3B)	1965	Spike Lundberg (P)	2006
Steve Lembo (C)	1950–52	Dolf Luque (P)	1930–31
Ed Lennox (3B)	1909–10	Barry Lyons (C)	1990–91
Dutch Leonard (P)	1933–36	Jim Lyttle (OF)	1976
Jeffrey Leonard (OF)	1977		
Sam Leslie (1B)	1933–35	**M**	
Dennis Lewallyn (P)	1975–79	Ed MacGamwell (1B)	1905
Darren Lewis (OF)	1997	Max Macon (P)	1940–43
Phil Lewis (SS)	1905–08	Greg Maddux (P)	2006
Jim Leyritz (C)	2000	Mike Maddux (P)	1990, 1999–2000
Bob Lillis (SS)	1958–61	Bill Madlock (3B)	1985–87
Jose Lima (P)	2004	Lee Magee (OF)	1919
Jim Lindsey (P)	1937	Sal Maglie (P)	1956–57
Freddie Lindstrom (3B)	1936	George Magoon (SS)	1898
Nelson Liriano (2B)	1996–97	Pat Mahomes (P)	2005
Mickey Livingston (C)	1951	Duster Mails (P)	1915–16
Scott Livingstone (3B)	1998–99	Charlie Malay (2B)	1905
Paul Lo Duca (C)	1998–2004	Candy Maldonado (OF)	1981–85
Billy Loes (P)	1950–56	Tony Malinosky (3B)	1937
Kenny Lofton (OF)	2006	Mal Mallette (P)	1950
Dick Loftus (OF)	1924–25	Christopher Malone (P)	2006
Bob Logan (P)	1935	Lew Malone (3B)	1917–19
Bill Lohrman (P)	1943–44	Billy Maloney (OF)	1906–08
Ernie Lombardi (C)	1931	Sean Maloney (P)	1998
Vic Lombardi (P)	1945–47	Al Mamaux (P)	1918–23
James Loney (1B)	2006	Gus Mancuso (C)	1940
Tom Long (P)	1924	Charlie Manuel (OF)	1974–75
Davey Lopes (2B)	1972–81	Heinie Manush (OF)	1937–38
Al Lopez (C)	1928–35	Rabbit Maranville (SS)	1926
Luis Lopez (C)	1990	Juan Marichal (P)	1975
Charlie Loudenslager (2B)	1904	Rube Marquard (P)	1915–20
Tom Lovett (P)	1889–93	Oreste Marrero (1B)	1996
Derek Lowe (P)	2005–06	William Marriott (3B)	1926–27
Ray Lucas (P)	1933–34	Buck Marrow (P)	1937–38
Con Lucid (P)	1894–95	Doc Marshall (C)	1909

Mike Marshall (P)	1974–76	Joe McGinnity (P)	1900
Mike Marshall (OF)	1981–89	Pat McGlothin (P)	1949–50
Morrie Martin (P)	1949	Bob McGraw (P)	1925–27
Russell Martin (C)	2006	Fred McGriff (1B)	2003
Tom Martin (P)	2003–04	Deacon McGuire (C)	1899, 1900–01
Pedro Martinez (P)	1992–93	Harry McIntire (P)	1905–09
Ramon Martinez (P)	1988–98, 2000–01	Doc McJames (P)	1899–1901
Ramon Martinez (SS)	2006	Kit McKenna (P)	1898
Ted Martinez (SS)	1977–79	Ed McLane (OF)	1907
Onan Masaoka (P)	1999–2001	Cal McLish (P)	1944–46
Earl Mattingly (P)	1931	Sadie McMahon (P)	1897
Len Matuszek (1B)	1985–87	John McMakin (P)	1902
Gene Mauch (2B)	1944, 1948	Frank McManus (C)	1903
Al Maul (P)	1899	Greg McMichael (P)	1998
Ralph Mauriello (P)	1958	Tommy McMillan (SS)	1908–10
Carmen Mauro (OF)	1953	Ken McMullen (3B)	1962–64, 1973–75
Brent Mayne (C)	2004	Jim McTamany (OF)	1885–87
Al Mays (P)	1888	George McVey (C)	1885
Al McBean (P)	1969, 1970	Doug McWeeny (P)	1926–29
Bill McCabe (OF)	1920	Brian Meadows (P)	2006
Gene McCann (P)	1901–02	Joe Medwick (OF)	1940–43, 1946
Bill McCarren (3B)	1923	Michael Megrew (P)	2006
Jack McCarthy (OF)	1906–07	Adam Melhuse (C)	2000
Johnny McCarthy (1B)	1934–35	Jonathan Meloan (P)	2006
Tommy McCarthy (OF)	1896	Rube Melton (P)	1943–47
Lew McCarty (C)	1913–16	Orlando Mercado (C)	1987
Jim McCauley (C)	1886	Fred Merkle (1B)	1916–17
Bill McClellan (2B)	1885–88	Andy Messersmith (P)	1973–75, 1979
Mike McCormick (3B)	1904	Mike Metcalfe (OF)	1994–2000
Mike McCormick (OF)	1949	Irish Meusel (OF)	1927
Walt McCredie (OF)	1903	Benny Meyer (OF)	1913
Tom McCreery (OF)	1901–03	Leo Meyer (SS)	1909
Terry McDermott (1B)	1972	Russ Meyer (P)	1953–55
Danny McDevitt (P)	1957, 1958–60	Chief Meyers (C)	1916–17
Sandy McDougal (P)	1895	Gene Michael (SS)	1967
Roger McDowell (P)	1991, 1992–94	Glenn Mickens (P)	1953
Pryor McElveen (3B)	1909–11	Pete Mikkelsen (P)	1969–72
Dan McFarlan (P)	1899	Eddie Miksis (2B)	1944–51
Chappie McFarland (P)	1906	Don Miles (OF)	1958
Dan McGann (1B)	1899	Johnny Miljus (P)	1917–21

Bob Miller (P)	1963–67
Fred Miller (P)	1910
Greg Miller (P)	2005–06
Hack Miller (OF)	1916
John Miller (OF)	1969
Larry Miller (P)	1964
Lemmie Miller (OF)	1984
Otto Miller (C)	1910–22
Ralph Miller (P)	1898
Trever Miller (P)	2000
Walt Miller (P)	1911
Wally Millies (C)	1934
Bob Milliken (P)	1953–54
Alan Mills (P)	1998–2000
Buster Mills (OF)	1935
Paul Minner (P)	1946–49
Bobby Mitchell (OF)	1980–81
Clarence Mitchell (P)	1918–22
Dale Mitchell (OF)	1956
Fred Mitchell (P)	1904–05
Johnny Mitchell (SS)	1924–25
Dave Mlicki (P)	1998–99
Joe Moeller (P)	1962–71
George Mohart (P)	1920–21
Rick Monday (OF)	1977–84
Raul Mondesi (OF)	1993–99
Wally Moon (OF)	1959–65
Cy Moore (P)	1929–32
Dee Moore (C)	1943
Eddie Moore (2B)	1929–30
Gary Moore (OF)	1970
Gene Moore (OF)	1939–40
Randy Moore (OF)	1936–37
Ray Moore (P)	1952–53
Jose Morales (DH)	1982–84
Herbie Moran (OF)	1912–13
Bobby Morgan (2B)	1950–53
Eddie Morgan (OF)	1937
Mike Morgan (P)	1989–91
Jim Morris Jr. (P)	2000

Johnny Morrison (P)	1929–30
Walt Moryn (OF)	1954–55
Ray Moss (P)	1926–31
Earl Mossor (P)	1951
Guillermo Mota (P)	2002–04
Manny Mota (OF)	1969–82
Glen Moulder (P)	1946
Ray Mowe (SS)	1913
Mike Mowrey (3B)	1916–17
Danny Muegge (P)	2006
Bill Mueller (3B)	2005–06
Terry Mulholland (P)	2001–02
Billy Mullen (3B)	1923
Scott Mullen (P)	2003
Joe Mulvey (3B)	1895
Van Mungo (P)	1931–41
Les Munns (P)	1934–35
Mike Munoz (P)	1989–90
Noe Munoz (C)	1995
Simmy Murch (2B)	1908
Rob Murphy (P)	1995
Eddie Murray (1B)	1989–91, 1997
Jim Murray (P)	1922
Hy Myers (OF)	1909–22
Rodney Myers (P)	2003–04
Brian Myrow (1B)	2005

N

Sam Nahem (P)	1938
Norihiro Nakamura (3B)	2005
Dan Naulty (P)	1999–2000
Dioner Navarro (C)	2005–06
Earl Naylor (OF)	1946
Charlie Neal (2B)	1956–61
Ron Negray (P)	1952, 1958
Jim Neidlinger (P)	1990
Bernie Neis (OF)	1920–24
Rocky Nelson (1B)	1952, 1956
Dick Nen (1B)	1963
Don Newcombe (P)	1949–58

Bobo Newsom (P)	1929–30, 1942–43
Warren Newson (OF)	1998–99
Doc Newton (P)	1901–02
Rod Nichols (P)	1993
Tom Niedenfuer (P)	1981–87
Otho Nitcholas (P)	1945
Al Nixon (OF)	1915–18
Otis Nixon (OF)	1997
Hideo Nomo (P)	1995–98, 2002–04
Jerry Nops (P)	1900
Irv Noren (OF)	1960
Fred Norman (P)	1970
Billy North (OF)	1978
Hub Northen (OF)	1911–12
Jose Nunez (P)	2001

O

Bob O'Brien (P)	1971
Jack O'Brien (C)	1887
John O'Brien (2B)	1891
Lefty O'Doul (OF)	1931–33
Ollie O'Mara (SS)	1914–19
Mickey O'Neil (C)	1926
Frank O'Rourke (3B)	1917–18
Johnny Oates (C)	1977–79
Whitey Ock (C)	1935
Joe Oeschger (P)	1925
Jose Offerman (SS)	1990–95
Bob Ojeda (P)	1991–92
Dave Oldfield (C)	1885–86
Al Oliver (OF)	1985
Nate Oliver (2B)	1963–67
Luis Olmo (OF)	1943–49
Gregg Olson (P)	2000–01
Ivy Olson (SS)	1915–24
Ralph Onis (C)	1935
Justin Orenduff (P)	2006
Joe Orengo (3B)	1943
Jesse Orosco (P)	1987–88
Jesse Orosco (P)	2001–02

Dave Orr (1B)	1888
Jorge Orta (2B)	1982
Phil Ortega (P)	1960–64
Tiny Osborne (P)	1924–25
Charlie Osgood (P)	1944
Franquelis Osoria (P)	2005–06
Claude Osteen (P)	1965–73
Fritz Ostermueller (P)	1943–44
Al Osuna (P)	1994
Antonio Osuna (P)	1995–2000
Billy Otterson (SS)	1887
Chink Outen (C)	1933
Mickey Owen (C)	1941–45
Red Owens (2B)	1905

P

Tom Paciorek (OF)	1970–75
Don Padgett (C)	1946
Andy Pafko (OF)	1951–52
Phil Page (P)	1934
Erv Palica (P)	1945–54
Ed Palmquist (P)	1960–61
Chan Ho Park (P)	1994–2001
Rick Parker (OF)	1995–96
Wes Parker (1B)	1964–72
Art Parks (OF)	1937–39
Jose Parra (P)	1995
Jay Partridge (2B)	1927–28
Camilo Pascual (P)	1970
Kevin Pasley (C)	1974–77
Jim Pastorius (P)	1906–09
Harry Pattee (2B)	1908
Dave Patterson (P)	1979
Jimmy Pattison (P)	1929
Xavier Paul (OF)	2006
Harley Payne (P)	1896–98
Johnny Peacock (C)	1945
Hal Peck (OF)	1943
Stu Pederson (OF)	1985
Alejandro Peña (P)	1981–89

Angel Peña (C)	1998–2001	Boog Powell (1B)	1977
Jose Peña (P)	1970–72	Dennis Powell (P)	1985–86
Brad Penny (P)	2004–06	Paul Powell (OF)	1973–75
Jimmy Peoples (C)	1885–88	Ted Power (P)	1981–82
Jack Perconte (2B)	1980–81	Tot Pressnell (P)	1938–40
Antonio Perez (3B)	2004–05	Tom Prince (C)	1993–98
Carlos Perez (P)	1998–2001	Luke Prokopec (P)	2000–01
Odalis Perez (P)	2002–06	John Purdin (P)	1964–69
Charlie Perkins (P)	1934	Eddie Pye (2B)	1994–95
Ron Perranoski (P)	1961–67, 1972		
Pat Perry (P)	1990	**Q**	
Jim Peterson (P)	1937	Paul Quantrill (P)	2002–03
Jesse Petty (P)	1925–28	Jack Quinn (P)	1931–32
Jeff Pfeffer (P)	1913–21		
George Pfister (C)	1941	**R**	
Lee Pfund (P)	1945	Steve Rachunok (P)	1940
Babe Phelps (C)	1935–41	Marv Rackley (OF)	1947–49
Ed Phelps (C)	1912–13	Paul Radford (OF)	1888
Ray Phelps (P)	1930–32	Scott Radinsky (P)	1996–98
Bill Phillips (1B)	1885–87	Jack Radtke (2B)	1936
Jason Phillips (C)	2005	Pat Ragan (P)	1911–15
Mike Piazza (C)	1992–98	Anthony Raglani (LF)	2006
Val Picinich (C)	1929–33	Ed Rakow (P)	1960
Joe Pignatano (C)	1957–60	Bob Ramazzotti (2B)	1946–49
Julio Pimentel (P)	2006	Willie Ramsdell (P)	1947–50
George Pinkney (3B)	1885–91	Mike Ramsey (2B)	1985
Ed Pipgras (P)	1932	Mike Ramsey (OF)	1987
Norman Plitt (P)	1918–27	Willie Randolph (2B)	1989–90
Bud Podbielan (P)	1949–52	Gary Rath (P)	1998
Johnny Podres (P)	1953–66	Doug Rau (P)	1972–79
Boots Poffenberger (P)	1939	Lance Rautzhan (P)	1977–79
Nick Polly (3B)	1937	Phil Reardon (OF)	1906
Ed Poole (P)	1904	Jeff Reboulet (2B)	2001–02
Jim Poole (P)	1990	Harry Redmond (2B)	1909
Paul Popovich (2B)	1968–69	Howie Reed (P)	1964–66
Henry Porter (P)	1885–87	Jody Reed (2B)	1993
Bill Posedel (P)	1938	Pee Wee Reese (SS)	1940–58
Sam Post (1B)	1922	Phil Regan (P)	1966–68
Dykes Potter (P)	1938	Bill Reidy (P)	1899, 1903–04
Bill Pounds (P)	1903	Bobby Reis (P)	1931–35

Pete Reiser (OF)	1940–48	Preacher Roe (P)	1948–54
Doc Reisling (P)	1904–05	Ed Roebuck (P)	1955–63
Jack Remsen (OF)	1884	Ron Roenicke (OF)	1981–83
Jason Repko (OF)	2005–06	Oscar Roettger (1B)	1927
Rip Repulski (OF)	1959–60	Lee Rogers (P)	1938
Ed Reulbach (P)	1913–14	Packy Rogers (SS)	1938
Jerry Reuss (P)	1979–87	Jimmy Rohan (1B)	2006
Al Reyes (P)	2000–01	Mel Rojas (P)	1999
Dennys Reyes (P)	1997–98	Stan Rojek (SS)	1942–47
Gil Reyes (C)	1983–88	Jason Romano (OF)	2003
Charlie Reynolds (C)	1889	Jim Romano (P)	1950
R.J. Reynolds (OF)	1983–85	Vicente Romo (P)	1968
Billy Rhiel (3B)	1929	Vicente Romo (P)	1982
Rick Rhoden (P)	1974–78	Mike Rose (C)	2005
Paul Richards (C)	1932	Johnny Roseboro (C)	1957–67
Danny Richardson (2B)	1893	Chief Roseman (OF)	1887
Pete Richert (P)	1962–64, 1972–73	Goody Rosen (OF)	1937–46
Harry Riconda (3B)	1928	Max Rosenfeld (OF)	1931–33
Joe Riggert (OF)	1914	Cody Ross (OF)	2005–06
Adam Riggs (2B)	1997	David Ross (C)	2002–04
Lew Riggs (3B)	1941–46	Don Ross (3B)	1940
Jimmy Ripple (OF)	1939–40	Ken Rowe (P)	1963
Lew Ritter (C)	1902–08	Schoolboy Rowe (P)	1942
German Rivera (3B)	1983–84	Jean-Pierre Roy (P)	1946
Johnny Rizzo (OF)	1942	Luther Roy (P)	1929
Dave Roberts (OF)	2002–04	Jerry Royster (3B)	1973–75
Jim Roberts (P)	1924–25	Wilkin Ruan (OF)	2002–06
Rick Roberts (P)	2003	Nap Rucker (P)	1907–16
Dick Robertson (P)	1918	Ernie Rudolph (P)	1945
Charlie Robinson (C)	1885	Dutch Ruether (P)	1921–24
Earl Robinson (OF)	1958	Justin Ruggiano (CF)	2006
Frank Robinson (OF)	1972	Andy Rush (P)	1925
Jackie Robinson (2B)	1947–56	Bill Russell (SS)	1969–86
Oscar Robles (SS)	2005–06	Jim Russell (OF)	1950–51
Sergio Robles (C)	1976	John Russell (P)	1917–18
Lou Rochelli (2B)	1944	Johnny Rutherford (P)	1952
Rich Rodas (P)	1983–84	Jack Ryan (C)	1898
Ellie Rodriguez (C)	1976	Jack Ryan (P)	1911
Felix Rodriguez (P)	1995	Rosy Ryan (P)	1933
Henry Rodriguez (OF)	1992–95		

S

Olmedo Saenz (1B)	2004–06	Dave Sells (P)	1975
Takashi Saito (P)	2006	Jae Seo (P)	2006
Juan Samuel (2B)	1990–92	Elmer Sexauer (P)	1948
Duaner Sanchez (P)	2004–05	Greg Shanahan (P)	1973–74
Mike Sandlock (C)	1945–46	Mike Sharperson (3B)	1987–93
Chance Sanford (3B)	1999–2000	George Sharrott (P)	1893–94
F.P. Santangelo (OF)	2000	Joe Shaute (P)	1931–1933
Jack Savage (P)	1987	Jeff Shaw (P)	1998–2001
Ted Savage (OF)	1968	Merv Shea (C)	1938
Dave Sax (C)	1982–83	Jimmy Sheckard (OF)	1897–98; 1900–05
Steve Sax (2B)	1981–88	Tommy Sheehan (3B)	1908
Bill Sayles (P)	1943	Jack Sheehan (SS)	1920–21
Doc Scanlan (P)	1904–11	Gary Sheffield (OF)	1998–2002
Bill Schardt (P)	1911–12	John Shelby (OF)	1987–90
Al Scheer (OF)	1913	Red Sheridan (SS)	1918–20
Bill Schenck (3B)	1885	Vince Sherlock (2B)	1935
Dutch Schliebner (1B)	1923	Larry Sherry (P)	1958–63
Ray Schmandt (1B)	1918–22	Norm Sherry (C)	1959–62
Henry Schmidt (P)	1903	Billy Shindle (3B)	1894–98
Johnny Schmitz (P)	1951–52	Craig Shipley (3B)	1986–87
Steve Schmoll (P)	2005	Bart Shirley (SS)	1964–66, 1968
Charlie Schmutz (P)	1914–15	Steve Shirley (P)	1982
Frank Schneiberg (P)	1910	George Shoch (OF)	1893–97
Dick Schofield (SS)	1966, 1967	Harry Shriver (P)	1922–23
Dick Schofield (SS)	1995	George Shuba (OF)	1948–55
Gene Schott (P)	1939	Paul Shuey (P)	2002–04
Paul Schreiber (P)	1922–23	Dick Siebert (1B)	1932–36
Pop Schriver (C)	1886	Ed Silch (OF)	1888
Howie Schultz (1B)	1943–47	Joe Simpson (OF)	1975–78
Joe Schultz (OF)	1915	Duke Sims (C)	1971–72
Ferdie Schupp (P)	1921	Bill Singer (P)	1964–72
Mike Scioscia (C)	1980–92	Fred Sington (OF)	1938–39
Dick Scott (P)	1963	Ted Sizemore (2B)	1969–70, 1976
Rudy Seanez (P)	1994–95	Frank Skaff (1B)	1935
Ray Searage (P)	1989–90	Bill Skowron (1B)	1963
Tom Seats (P)	1945	Gordon Slade (SS)	1930–32
Jimmy Sebring (OF)	1909	Lefty Sloat (P)	1948
Larry See (1B)	1986	Aleck Smith (C)	1897–1900
Aaron Sele (P)	2006	Charley Smith (3B)	1960–61
		Dick Smith (OF)	1965

George Smith (P)	1918, 1923	Scott Stewart (P)	2004
Germany Smith (SS)	1885–90, 1897	Stuffy Stewart (2B)	1923
Greg Smith (2B)	1991	Bob Stinson (C)	1969–70
Happy Smith (OF)	1910	Milt Stock (3B)	1924–26
Jack Smith (P)	1962–63	Harry Stovey (OF)	1893
Phenomenal Smith (P)	1885	Mike Strahler (P)	1970–72
Red Smith (3B)	1911–14	Sammy Strang (3B)	1903–04
Reggie Smith (OF)	1976–81	Joe Strauss (OF)	1886
Sherry Smith (P)	1915–22	Darryl Strawberry (OF)	1991–93
Tony Smith (SS)	1910–11	Elmer Stricklett (P)	1905–07
Red Smyth (OF)	1915–17	Joe Stripp (3B)	1932–37
Harry Smythe (P)	1934	Dutch Stryker (P)	1926
Duke Snider (OF)	1947–62	Dick Stuart (1B)	1966
Gene Snyder (P)	1959	Franklin Stubbs (1B)	1984–89
Jack Snyder (C)	1917	Eric Stults (P)	2006
Cory Snyder (OF)	1993–94	Bill Sudakis (3B)	1968–71
Eddie Solomon (P)	1973–74	Clyde Sukeforth (C)	1932–45
Andy Sommerville (P)	1894	Billy Sullivan (C)	1942
Elias Sosa (P)	1976–77	Tom Sunkel (P)	1944
Denny Sothern (OF)	1931	Rick Sutcliffe (P)	1976–81
Roy Spencer (C)	1937–38	Don Sutton (P)	1966–80, 1988
Daryl Spencer (SS)	1961–63	Ed Swartwood (OF)	1885–87
Karl Spooner (P)	1954–55	Bill Swift (P)	1941
Dennis Springer (P)	2001–02		
Eddie Stack (P)	1912–13	**T**	
Tuck Stainback (OF)	1938–39	Vito Tamulis (P)	1938–41
George Stallings (C)	1890	Kevin Tapani (P)	1995
Jerry Standaert (2B)	1925–26	Tommy Tatum (OF)	1941–47
Don Stanhouse (P)	1980	Alex Taveras (2B)	1982–83
Eddie Stanky (2B)	1944–47	Danny Taylor (OF)	1932–36
Dolly Stark (SS)	1910–12	Harry Taylor (P)	1946–48
Jigger Statz (OF)	1927–28	Zack Taylor (C)	1920–25, 1935
Elmer Steele (P)	1911	Chuck Templeton (P)	1955–56
Bill Steele (P)	1914	Joe Tepsic (OF)	1946
Farmer Steelman (C)	1900–01	Adonis Terry (P)	1884–91
Ed Stein (P)	1892–98	Wayne Terwilliger (2B)	1951
Casey Stengel (OF)	1912–17	Grant Thatcher (P)	1903–04
Jerry Stephenson (P)	1970	Nick Theodorou (2B)	2004
Ed Stevens (1B)	1945–47	Henry Thielman (P)	1903
Dave Stewart (P)	1978-1983	Derrel Thomas (2B)	1979–83

Fay Thomas (P)	1932	Bobby Valentine (SS)	1969–72
Ray Thomas (C)	1938	Fernando Valenzuela (P)	1980–90
Gary Thomasson (OF)	1979–80	Hector Valle (C)	1965
Derek Thompson (P)	2005	Elmer Valo (OF)	1957–58
Don Thompson (OF)	1951–54	Chris Van Cuyk (P)	1950–52
Fresco Thompson (2B)	1931–32	Johnny Van Cuyk (P)	1947–49
Jason Thompson (1B)	1998–99	Deacon Vanburen (OF)	1904
Milt Thompson (OF)	1996	Dazzy Vance (P)	1922–32, 1935
Tim Thompson (C)	1954	Sandy Vance (P)	1970–71
Hank Thormahlen (P)	1925	Ed Vande Berg (P)	1986
Joe Thurston (2B)	2002–04	Arky Vaughan (SS)	1942–48
Sloppy Thurston (P)	1930–33	Mike Venafro (P)	2004
Cotton Tierney (2B)	1925	Robin Ventura (3B)	2003–04
Al Todd (C)	1939	Zoilo Versalles (SS)	1968
Brett Tomko (P)	2005–06	Rube Vickers (P)	1903
Steve Toole (P)	1886–87	Joe Visner (OF)	1889
Bert Tooley (SS)	1911–12	Jose Vizcaino (SS)	1989–90, 1998–2000
Jeff Torborg (C)	1964–70	Joe Vosmik (OF)	1940–41
Dick Tracewski (SS)	1962–65		
Brian Traxler (1B)	1990	**W**	
George Treadway (OF)	1894–95	Paul Wachtel (P)	1917
Jeff Treadway (2B)	1994–95	Ben Wade (P)	1952–54
Nick Tremark (OF)	1934–36	Bull Wagner (P)	1913–14
Overton Tremper (OF)	1927–28	Butts Wagner (3B)	1898
Alex Trevino (C)	1986–87	Dixie Walker (OF)	1939–47
Ricky Trlicek (P)	1993	Mysterious Walker (P)	1913
Mike Trombley (P)	2001–02	Oscar Walker (OF)	1884
Chris Truby (3B)	2005–06	Rube Walker (C)	1951–58
Tommy Tucker (1B)	1898	Joe Wall (C)	1902
John Tudor (P)	1988–89	Stan Wall (P)	1975–77
Ty Tyson (OF)	1928	Tim Wallach (3B)	1993–96
		Lee Walls (OF)	1962–64
U		Dave Walsh (P)	1990
Fred Underwood (P)	1894	Danny Walton (OF)	1976
		Lloyd Waner (OF)	1944
V		Paul Waner (OF)	1941, 1943–44
Mike Vail (OF)	1984	Chuck Ward (SS)	1918–22
Ismael Valdez (P)	1994–2000	Daryle Ward (OF)	2003
Rene Valdez (P)	1957	John Ward (SS)	1891–92
Jose Valentin (SS)	2005	Preston Ward (1B)	1948

Rube Ward (OF)	1902	Rick Wilkins (C)	1999
Fred Warner (3B)	1884	Nick Willhite (P)	1963–66
Jack Warner (3B)	1929–31	Dick Williams (OF)	1951–54, 1956
Tommy Warren (P)	1944	Eddie Williams (1B)	1997
Carl Warwick (OF)	1961	Jeff Williams (P)	1999–2002
Jimmy Wasdell (OF)	1940–41	Leon Williams (P)	1926
Ron Washington (SS)	1977	Reggie Williams (OF)	1985–87, 1995
George Watkins (OF)	1936	Stan Williams (P)	1958–62
Gary Wayne (P)	1994	Todd Williams (P)	1995
Eric Weaver (P)	1998	Woody Williams (2B)	1938
Jeff Weaver (P)	2004–05	Maury Wills (SS)	1959–66, 1969, 1970–72
Hank Webb (P)	1977	Bob Wilson (OF)	1958
Les Webber (P)	1942–46	Eddie Wilson (OF)	1936–37
Jon Weber (RF)	2005–06	Hack Wilson (OF)	1932–34
Mitch Webster (OF)	1991–95	Steve Wilson (P)	1991–93
Gary Weiss (SS)	1980–81	Tex Wilson (P)	1924
Bob Welch (P)	1978–87	Tom Wilson (C)	2004
Brad Wellman (2B)	1987	Tug Wilson (OF)	1884
John Wells (P)	1944	Gordie Windhorn (OF)	1961
Terry Wells (P)	1990	Jim Winford (P)	1938
Johnny Werhas (3B)	1964–65, 1967	Lave Winham (P)	1902
Jayson Werth (OF)	2004–06	Tom Winsett (OF)	1936–38
Max West (OF)	1928–29	Hank Winston (P)	1936
John Wetteland (P)	1989–91	Whitey Witt (OF)	1926
Gus Weyhing (P)	1900	Pete Wojey (P)	1954
Mack Wheat (C)	1915–19	Tracy Woodson (3B)	1987–89
Zack Wheat (OF)	1909–26	Todd Worrell (P)	1993–97
Ed Wheeler (3B)	1902	Gene Wright (P)	1901
Matt Whisenant (P)	2000	Glenn Wright (SS)	1929–33
Barney White (3B)	1945	Ricky Wright (P)	1982–83
Devon White (OF)	1998–2001	Zeke Wrigley (SS)	1899
Larry White (P)	1983–84	Kelly Wunsch (P)	2005–06
Myron White (OF)	1978	Frank Wurm (P)	1944
Terry Whitfield (OF)	1984–86	Whit Wyatt (P)	1939–44
Jesse Whiting (P)	1906–07	Jimmy Wynn (OF)	1974–75
Dick Whitman (OF)	1946–49		
Possum Whitted (OF)	1922	**Y**	
Kemp Wicker (P)	1941	Ad Yale (1B)	1905
Hoyt Wilhelm (P)	1971–72	Rube Yarrison (P)	1924
Kaiser Wilhelm (P)	1908–10	Joe Yeager (3B)	1898–1900

Steve Yeager (C)	1972–85	Pat Zachry (P)	1983–84
Earl Yingling (P)	1912–13	Geoff Zahn (P)	1973–75
Delwyn Young (OF)	2005–06	Todd Zeile (3B)	1997–98
Eric Young (2B)	1992, 1997–99	Don Zimmer (3B)	1954–59, 1963
Matt Young (P)	1987	Bill Zimmerman (OF)	1915
		Eddie Zimmerman (3B)	1911

Z

Chink Zachary (P)	1944
Tom Zachary (P)	1934–36

Notes

"He That Will Not Reason Is a Bigot"

"I don't see why you can't come up with a Negro," McLaughlin heartily agreed... Chalberg, John C., *Rickey and Robinson*, Harlan Davidson, 2000.

"I Want a Player with the Guts Not to Fight Back!"

"I get it," he said. "I've got another cheek..." Stout, Glenn and Richard A. Johnson, *The Dodgers: 120 Years of Dodgers Baseball*, New York: Houghton Mifflin, 2004.

The Good Samaritan

He is a hero in L.A. because his selfish decisions benefited his new city, but O'Malley reminds one of a famous quote by a wise man who said, "What you do is so loud I cannot hear what you say." Snider, Duke and Phil Pepe, *Few and Chosen: Defining Dodgers Greatness Across the Eras*, Chicago: Triumph Publishing, 2006.

Breaking into the Big Leagues

"I wasn't sure if my teammates would shake my hand," he said, breathing a sigh of relief, while also revealing his human frailty, a trait that helped make him a sympathetic figure... Chalberg, John C., *Rickey and Robinson*, Harlan Davidson, 2000.

"I'm going to meet my maker someday, and if he asks me why I didn't let this boy play and I say it's because he's black, that might not be a satisfactory answer," he told Rickey... Stout, Glenn and Richard A. Johnson, *The Dodgers: 120 Years of Dodgers Baseball*, New York: Houghton Mifflin, 2004.

"The Shot Heard 'Round the World"

Durocher did tell him, "If you ever hit one, hit one now." Stout, Glenn and Richard A. Johnson, *The Dodgers: 120 Years of Dodgers Baseball*, New York: Houghton Mifflin, 2004.

Still "Waiting Till Next Year"

"If we can pull this out," Leo Durocher said, "there'll be 100,000 suicides in Brooklyn." Stout, Glenn and Richard A. Johnson, *The Dodgers: 120 Years of Dodgers Baseball*, New York: Houghton Mifflin, 2004.

Team Leader

"It was fun," he said. "I didn't know what adversity was in baseball when I was a youngster..." Snider, Duke and Phil Pepe, *Few and Chosen: Defining Dodgers Greatness Across the Eras*, Chicago: Triumph Publishing, 2006.

Changes

"If it hadn't been for the accident," Snider once said, "I think Roy would have played another year or two and then been the first black manager." Travers, Steven, "Changes," *StreetZebra*, May 1999.

The Real "Dr. K"

It was Drysdale's turn on three days' rest. Alston was concerned about hurting Big D's pride, but Drysdale just told Alston, "If I was the manager, I'd pitch Sandy. I'll be ready. I'll go down to the bullpen and I'll be ready if something happens, but I'd pitch him too." Stout, Glenn and Richard A. Johnson, *The Dodgers: 120 Years of Dodgers Baseball*, New York: Houghton Mifflin, 2004.

Big D

Drysdale was "one of the finest competitors I have ever known," according to Duke Snider... Snider, Duke and Phil Pepe, *Few and Chosen: Defining Dodgers Greatness Across the Eras*, Chicago: Triumph Publishing, 2006.

Pride Goeth before the Fall
Oakland captain Sal Bando then suggested to outfielder Reggie Jackson, "Buck, I suggest we dispose of these people as quickly as possible..." Jackson, Reggie and Mike Lupica, *Reggie*, New York: Ballantine Books, 1984.

The Last Hurrah
By this time, just getting a hit off the man almost seemed worthy of headlines the same size as, say, "Kennedy Murder Solved" or "Osama in Custody." Travers, Steven, "The Dodgers' Last Hurrah," *StreetZebra*, October 1999.

Piazza
"I guarantee you, this kid will hit the ball," Williams told Vince. Stout, Glenn and Richard A. Johnson, *The Dodgers: 120 Years of Dodgers Baseball*, New York: Houghton Mifflin, 2004.

The Poet
"We just needed somebody to sort of take an inning here and there and just do little things," Scully told Gary Kaufman. salon.com.